The Apocalypse of the Mind

Transforming Ego into Stillness of Consciousness

The Apocalypse of the Mind

Transforming Ego into Stillness of Consciousness

Melissa Lowe, Ph.D.

BOOKS

Winchester, UK
Washington, USA

First published by O-Books, 2011
O Books is an imprint of John Hunt Publishing Ltd., The Bothy, Deershot Lodge, Park Lane, Ropley,
Hants, SO24 0BE, UK
office1@o-books.net
www.o-books.com

For distributor details and how to order please visit the 'Ordering' section on our website.

Text copyright Melissa Lowe 2010

www.melissalowe.com

ISBN: 978 1 84694 430 7

A CIP catalogue record for this book is available from the British Library.

Design: Stuart Davies

Printed in the UK by CPI Antony Rowe
Printed in the USA by Offset Paperback Mfrs, Inc

We operate a distinctive and ethical publishing philosophy in all
areas of its business, from its global network of authors to
production and worldwide distribution.

CONTENTS

This book is in dedication to Dr. Brugh Joy.

In 1984, I had a chance encounter with an author and teacher in an obscured bookstore in Indiana. The result of this encounter is the author, Dr. Brugh Joy would introduce me to a world that was unlike my current reality. Standing at the threshold to an intriguing world of awakened awareness and seeing reality as energy, this man invited me with a smile and wave of his hand to explore with him the Great Mystery of Life. Brugh re-awakened within me my dormant interest and passion of psychology, the wonderment of heart centered awareness, the divine unconditional love and compassion as well as the multiple aspects of the psyche.

Dr. Joy was a humble teacher, who understood the art of sacrifice of ego, being in vulnerability and the value these two elements brought to psychological transformation. Yet, the rare gift of this teacher was his ability to allow his students to witness his visible vulnerability as he shared his life's journey and struggles. Brugh continued to reveal his journey even after discovering the return of pancreatic carcinoma by exposing his vulnerability, the ego conflicts and the awe and wonderment as he encountered his illness until his death in December, 2009. And so, I dedicate this book to the teacher that once guided many and to the man who once inspired many, may his teachings continue.

Acknowledgments

I express my gratitude to Laurie Schmidt, Tom Swartz, Pam, Liam and Jesse who encouraged me to begin and continue with this work. Their support assisted me during long hours of writing and editing. They reminded me more than once this work would be beneficial to others and needed.

Support and encouragement came from dear friends, Lynn Barlow and Gloria Friemoth who provided me with stimulating conversations and discussions, challenging me to become clearer in my approach to consciousness practice and theory. In addition, I appreciated the encouragement from Gary Helmke, who supported me in taking on such an endeavor. I am indebted to each one.

I also want to thank James Townsend, who not only provided editing advice but also gave invaluable comments during the initial stages of this project.

I am especially indebted to Leigh Westerfield who assisted me with the editing process from the initial drafts to final manuscript. It was her help, every step of the way, from the rough draft to the publishing stage that brought this project to completion. Without the assistance of her support and writing skills this book would not exist.

Preface

It is not often that a visit to the dentist changes one's entire perspective on life. But that is exactly what happened to me one momentous day in 2006.

Everything was normal. I was terrified, of course, of getting a tooth pulled, but I was relieved when it came out . . . right up to the moment I heard the dentist say, 'Will you look at the roots on this thing? Hey, your bone appears healthy.'

Then I passed out.

For only a few seconds, I left the anxiety-laden reality of the dentist's office. But, I was in an alternate reality for what seemed like hours. It was dark and chaotic. Nothing in this place had a solid physicality about it. Objects and people had a transparent, shadow-like quality. No day or night marked the passing of time. In this state of awareness, humans were just shadowy figures on the periphery of my vision, going about their lives, working at jobs, raising families, loving, laughing, keeping busy, and having their dramas.

I observed the activity of humanity around me, a perspective that was separate from everyone, yet a part of this other world. While I could only watch individuals within the span of my vision, I had a sense that this was the norm for most people in the world, this 'busy-ness' of activity. All of this hustle and bustle, which was no different from our ordinary reality, was occurring around me, but there was more.

Something large, chaotic, and undifferentiated was approaching. I sensed it was huge, a force, like a world-engulfing tsunami of energy. It was going to overwhelm us with its power, disorder, and unfamiliarity, as if we were in the midst of a tornado. Only it would affect our minds. No one took notice or was preparing for the arrival of this energy, though. The busy, drama-filled events of life distracted everyone and this energy was going to overtake them, unawares.

Deep within myself, I realized that the unfocused, distracted, dramatic way people were living their lives served a purpose: it kept them oblivious to what was coming, and therefore prevented overwhelming anxiety from taking control. However, because they were unaware, they also were unprepared for this force that was to bring with it a cataclysmic change. In contrast, though, I was focused and aware in this alternate reality. I sharply understood the pure function of ego, a state of focused consciousness, centered in its relationship to forces as yet unmanifested in thought or form, a witness and anchoring of my perceived orientation. How would one have even a glimpse of these forces and not be destroyed by their realization into consciousness?

Then, suddenly, I saw myself standing on a precipice of a vast void, on the verge of toppling over. I felt I was at the edge of losing my mind, losing my ability to track happenings in the moment . . . and if I entered the void I would have entered insanity. At that instant, the dentist called my name, bringing me sharply back into this reality and into some form of sanity and control under the egis of my ego.

I returned, disoriented, to my ordinary state of reality. Whether I had experienced a dream, another interpretation of reality, or a prophetic event, it gave me an instant understanding of the role that ego plays in the times in which we are living and what occurs when we transform ego. Ego is a tool that we use to pinpoint time and space, allowing us to have order, going beyond the surface or personality awareness, which is only a subset of ego. It sets up defensive structures against tsunami-like forces enabling us to retain some sanity. By having this resource of ego, we can focus in on a particular reality and this can allow a transformation of consciousness as well as our ego. An undeveloped adult ego though, becomes overwhelmed with fear and then defends and distracts. This serves a great purpose in keeping sanity when we don't have the inner resources or the timing of developmental dynamics that activate full conscious awareness are not in place. This experience ignited within me the desire to reflect on ego, consciousness, and the reshaping of both, as well as on their relationship to suffering.

The ego has to encounter the simultaneously destructive and creative life force within us at every moment, in the process of transforming consciousness. This was what occurred in the 'tsunami' of my alternate-reality experience. To be present in the moment, vulnerable and open to change and the creative force is like the experience I had standing at the edge of the void: a surrendering into something large and although unknowing of what will occur with this surrender, aware of its force. I am transfixed in awe of the processes of ego in its ability to subordinate and be the carrier of the Self and the Self's destiny, balancing between distraction, inflation or victimization of defense and the other alternative, insanity.

Apocalyptic Times

I have titled this book, *The Apocalypse of the Mind: Transforming Ego into Stillness of Consciousness*. It is a title that fits the times in which we live and also the tasks required in post-ego development, which I describe as the integration of consciousness. Integrative Consciousness is the process that allows us to live in stillness, in the full awareness of the moment, without the distractions that life offers up to keep us from becoming so fearful that we topple into insanity. This is a developmental stage that occurs successfully once a person has developed ego strength, which is one of the last tasks of the maturation of the ego, hence, the term that refers to development beyond this last task: post-ego development.

This book provides the resources to assist an individual with the process of Integrative Consciousness, which prepares and develops the ego so that it can be in relationship with the destructive and the creative life forces that are occurring both in the world as well as within the individual's life. This process allows a person to dramatically alter the parts of the ego that are heavily defended and fear-based, bringing them instead into a state of stillness and serenity. Integrative Consciousness prepares the individual to be in the 'tsunami,' much like my alternate reality experience, and to allow what needs to occur, without the toppling over into insanity or the heavily defended, unaware state of mind.

Why the title *The Apocalypse of the Mind*? The word apocalypse derives from the Greek *apok'lypsis*, meaning 'revelation,' which is equivalent to *apokalyptein*, referring to the 'uncovering of what has been hidden.' 'Apocalypse' invokes thoughts of chaos, punishment, terror, and upheaval, in other words, the breaking down of structures to reveal what has previously not been visible. While such events—which most people consider to be dark—occur in an apocalyptic situation, there is also the momentous coming of the Self, a Saving Grace, or, at collective levels, a 'Messiah' or 'Divine King,' signifying a new light-filled way of life and the dawn of a new era. This occurrence is the transformation from darkness to light. Typically, an apocalyptic moment in a person's life is the end of the life he / she once knew and a preparation or laying of the foundation for the new life to take root. Importantly, there is a difference between 'catastrophic' and 'apocalyptic.' With a catastrophe, there arises no new way of living but rather only devastation and the return and re-cycling of old patterns. With an apocalypse, on the other hand, what existed before is gone, and a new, greater order results. We are redeemed.

The more I have explored my own ego and consciousness, the more I have realized how apocalyptic in nature is this post-ego development. On an individual level, the coming of the enlightened Self contains all the chaos, destruction, the *under-world*—the blackening of forces that break down structures and form—as described above. But, there is a difference. When one continues to strive through chaos and devastation and is able to see that major change is afoot, the strife is overshadowed by the redeeming quality of the outcome and the realization of an expanded mind and a compassionate heart. The quality of our experiences are heightened. This, therefore, becomes an apocalyptic event in the individual's life.

This effort to attain transformation is serious and vital work, but it is often forgotten as we become distracted by inconsequential things in our lives, by others' dramas as well as our own, and by the need for a feeling of power and security that comes during times of transition. Often we deal with our insecurities by living a façade of socially accepted spirituality, and by living through our careers or families. But by appropriating power to an insecure and unstable surface ego, we prevent post-ego development, as well as hinder the deep transformative work required in these times. How do we know our life is one of insecurity? We ask ourselves if the decisions surrounding the life we are living are ones that arose out of fear and are we not moving toward our life of passion also out of fear?

The need to alter consciousness applies not only to the individual but also to the broader community at large. As the world collective moves toward increasingly difficult times, individual psychological transformation is a welcomed approach that enables us to face challenges and seek solutions for all of humankind. Collective change can only occur when enough individuals have transformed. This requires individuals to be present and quiet with fear, to be focused in moment-to-moment living, to remain undistracted by collective and individual fears, and to resist reaching for the subtle or extreme illusions of power that are reflected in our outer world. These are qualities becoming more and more essential as the world heads into earth-shaking apocalyptic events.

By perceiving the patterns at work around us, we can discern the tasks at hand. Until the late twentieth century, Americans believed in and relied upon the institutions that were in place to maintain the quality of life and security that we had come to expect. We trusted churches to give us moral guidance, businesses to provide our essential comforts and financial security, and government to oversee our social and individual liberties, to maintain order, and protect our interests and freedoms at home and abroad.

But in the 1990s, we began to witness the destruction of these esteemed structures to which we had indolently given over our power. The Catholic Church's transgressions, in the form of sexual abuse of altar boys by Church leaders, eroded America's faith in the Church's ability to give religious guidance. Other religious denominations soon followed with scandals of their own involving duplicity among church leaders—greed, sexual misconduct, and other moral offenses.

Corporations such as Enron and WorldCom, whom we had trusted to provide essentials in the form of communications, electricity, and power, were discovered to be dishonest in their business dealings, financially raping the communities and people they purportedly served, as well as those with vested interests in the products they provided.

Cult groups centered on charismatic characters—David Koresh, Charles Manson, Jim Jones, Rev. Sun Myung Moon, to name just a few—had already taken root in American culture. These cults represented group possession, requiring from their members complete obedience and the surrender of individual free will to the group leaders. Today, other smaller, less organized organizations of survivalists are currently living 'off of the grid,' awaiting Armageddon.

In 2001, we watched in horror as terrorists attacked our nation's symbols of financial strength, capitalism, commerce, banking, and free trade. The World Trade Center fell in the first-ever attack on America's mainland. Also assaulted that day were the symbols of our military power and the 'keepers of our freedom,' the Pentagon. Hatred toward our democracy was expressed through the terrorists' thwarted attack on the White House. We watched as the President rose to carry and champion the anger of a wounded and fearful nation, only to leave office in disgrace a few short years later with the lowest approval ratings of any American President, shaking the faith the American people had in this office.

In 1999, the Mighty Wizards of Wall Street, as well as other financial, banking, and investment institutions began to operate on the basis of greed as the government deregulated the banking and investment industry. The need for more and quicker profits, as well as the daily trading without the support of solid financial backing began to override these entities' ability to provide the consumer with sound consulting services. Americans believed they could easily achieve the American dream, guilelessly buying into the deals these institutions offered, purchasing homes they were unable to afford, until both the individual and major financial organizations were brought to ruin in 2008. We watched as the manufacturing industry, an industry that had once represented the innovative nature of American business and that had made America the leader of nations in the world of capitalism—an industry many people once thought invincible— downsized and closed the doors of new plants. The mismanaged automobile manufacturer GM finally declared bankruptcy in 2009.

The Task of the Conscious Individual
Not many of these masculine structures have escaped the uprising of their collective unconsciousness baring the under-bellies of their organizations. Many of us would easily classify these events as catastrophic, as they have led to not only the demise of a nation's infrastructure that holds in its safekeeping the individual's quality of life, but they also have had devas-

tating repercussions worldwide. But maybe what we think of as catastrophic in nature has at its underpinnings the elements of an apocalyptic process. The determining factor, the wild card, the unknown ingredient is the ability, first of individuals and then of the collective, to be present with fear and reach for transpersonal states of awareness to see clearly. In order to transform the possibility of catastrophe into apocalyptic probability, individuals and the collective must stay focused in the midst of the chaos, be fully aware (mind and body), find the stillness within, and allow what needs to be destroyed to no longer exist. Only then can they co-create the new order.

These events are challenging the individual to make those psychological or ego transformations required to find solutions and not become lost in the insanity of the world. As this is addressed on an individual level, it becomes the change agent on a collective level. We, as a collective, are responsible for not blindly turning over our power and the ownership of our livelihoods to large governing institutions or people. The task before us is to move beyond the parental / child relational level of functioning and the expectation of being taken care of by these agencies. The exploration of these forces that underlie the corruption of these agencies appears to reveal that what is being asked to transform, to be birthed, is that agencies, government, corporations, be of service to the many and not the continuing order of the many at service to the one.

As individuals, we are now being asked to live a more enlightened existence, with structures that a society needs in order to maintain a civil and rich way of living. We are challenged to understand clearly our beliefs and relationships around greed, entitlement, dependency, trust, betrayal, and fear of the unexpected and the unknown.

Are there signs of the redeeming quality that is intrinsic to an apocalyptic moment? Yes, the seeds of this transformation are already apparent. The election of an African-American president whose platform carried the message 'Yes, we can,' has begun to instill in us the role and responsibility each individual must take to face the challenges. There is the beginning of a movement that suggests that we are not willing to have one man in power to be responsible for making the decisions that a majority do not agree with. People seem to be no longer willing to take at face value what has been called 'the truth', but instead are beginning to look beneath the surface. More people are saying it is not good for us to be distracted by dramas and the insignificant happenings in the media, such as which star is sleeping with a certain actor, but rather that we must remain focused on the real problems at hand. These are indications that many of us are ready to take on the mantle of adulthood and partnership in times of challenge. Yet the question arises, is it enough to influence a collective and to direct change into an apocalyptic event?

In order to move as a collective, the individual must face the personal, fear-evoking dynamics that surface as we explore our relationship to what lies beneath the happenings of the last two decades—greed, power, irresponsibility, dependency, trust, betrayal, safety, and security. We must convert these dynamics from fear-based to love-based within ourselves, integrating into a different state of consciousness and a new pattern of living. Then will we be able to see through the illusions so that, as deceptions arise, we see; as greed arises, we see; as insecurity arises, we see. And then we move with compassion—with our companions and our experiences—until we are shown the new order of the new era.

The purpose of this book is to provide those individuals who want to awaken consciously with the resources and tools to help them read their unconscious and uncover what is hidden. These resources and tools will give readers the ability to discern their relationships to these dynamics of greed and power as well as to past sufferings. Such a person will discover herein how not to allow distraction as he / she remains aware of and present and unfaltering with fear or suffering, long enough to allow a new order to arise within him- or herself. Then, the task is to live with the strength, courage, and compassion that will influence the collective.

Can we as a collective redeem the catastrophic happenings of the end of this age to establish an apocalyptic new age for future generations? My experience as a consciousness therapist tells me that indeed we can. I have worked with consciousness techniques and have successfully applied these approaches to many challenging situations within my own life, as well as assisted individuals in my work as a mental health therapist and educator. In the chapters that follow, I provide personal stories along with reflective exercises and techniques that will allow the reader to awaken to a state of consciousness of living in the present moment with a stillness of mind.

Chapter 1

Now I Am Enlightened . . . Now I Am Not

We lead our lives so poorly because we arrive in the present always
unprepared, incapable, and too distracted for everything.

Rainer Marie Rilke, Letters to a Young Poet

What Is Enlightenment?

I have struggled with this question for most of my adult life. The
term enlightenment has been overused in recent years and
carries with it many misconceptions. Some people describe
enlightenment as a state of consciousness in which one has direct
experience of the true nature of life, transcends the ego, and
ceases the suffering of one's existence. In the Zen tradition,
enlightenment is seen as a possibility for everyone: the ability to
free oneself from beliefs, ideals, concepts, and opinions. In the
Indian Hindu traditions, enlightenment refers to an individual's
liberation from all of suffering and of the limitations of worldly
existence: it is a perfected state of consciousness. For other
Eastern religious belief systems, one attains enlightenment by
transcending ego and uncovering one's eternal identity. One
completely stills all material desires in order to enter into a state
of nirvana. Most Christian denominations view this perfected
state as one's relationship with God, an event in which an
individual receives the Grace of God by having Faith in God. The
philosopher Immanuel Kant approached enlightenment from a
Western philosophical viewpoint, believing that it occurs when a
person releases his / her need to rely on the guidance of another
and has the capacity to use his / her own understanding in
relating to the world.

I once subscribed to the notion of enlightenment as a state of

11

consciousness that leads to the ending of suffering, more of an Eastern philosophical perspective. Yet, I was unfamiliar with the meaning of these concepts of transcendence of the ego and the ending of suffering. These Eastern notions were too abstract for my Western intellect to grasp. Due to my own misinterpretation, lack of understanding, and naiveté about these beliefs, I encountered difficulties in my own awakening process. For example, when I was 25 years old, my early concept of enlightenment was to feel peace and compassion, to have no internal or external conflicts, to live without suffering, to feel a life-force energy pulsating through my body at all times, and, of course, to have everything I desired. In this quest for spiritual insight and a perfected state of being in the world, the peaceful and compassionate persona that I sought came at the price of the repression of vital aspects of my personality. It was as if being spiritual meant not having any anger, judgment, or fear, even though these feelings are valid emotions and important when one is on a spiritual path of discovery. I ignored internal conflictual feelings and thoughts. But by disregarding such thoughts and emotions, I actually missed the opportunities they presented that would have brought me into a present state of awareness.

Through my encounters over the years with others who desire this goal of transcendence, I believe that they also see enlightenment in this way. The very act of attempting or desiring to obtain this perfected state of consciousness creates additional ego suffering and a state of self-criticalness toward one's journey through life. One can avoid a great deal of angst by challenging one's own constructs around what it means to be enlightened.

By misinterpreting the concept of what enlightenment actually is, I developed obstacles to obtaining a deep sense of peace and happiness within myself. The struggles I encountered along this path of awareness became large and looming in their expressions. My idea of this perfected state of consciousness and of being in the world kept me longing for the realization of enlightenment, waiting for that lightening bolt to strike, when I would suddenly achieve this level of realization and be free of suffering. Without recognizing it, I had constructed a definition of enlightenment that was born of my ego, gathered from bits and pieces of teachings from people who had undergone some form of transformation or from teachers who purported to be enlightened themselves.

This initial concept of enlightenment set the bar of expectations too high for my own process of self-realization. The idea of a perfected state of awareness increased my struggle and kept me from obtaining a level of acceptance for myself as a valued person, as well as for my own journey and its natural unfolding, an unfolding that was unlike that of many of the self-proclaimed enlightened teachers whose work I would encounter. I struggled to release my suffering, yet no matter how long I meditated, attended seminars, and studied, enlightenment (that is, the end of suffering) was always beyond my grasp. I viewed the people who reported that they had reached enlightenment as people who lived extraordinary lives. I saw their existence as revolving around their spirituality. The journey of awareness became their work. In many cases, organizations and communities supported them in their practices of contemplation, meditation, and prayers, sequestering them from barriers that Western life can present. I regarded such individuals as having finished with suffering.

Escape from Suffering

I once heard a Buddhist parable that related to the notion of being sequestered away from the conflicts of the masses and thereby escaping suffering. This parable tells of a young man beginning his process of becoming a monk and moving to live in a monastery. He is concerned about removing himself from the world and the effects this will have on his attempts at uncovering his own ego suffering. Upon entering the monastery, he is given a robe, a metal bowl, and wooden spoon. These are his only belongings. These also are the only possessions given to all the other monks at the monastery. The young monk thinks that he will never have to worry about the evils of envy, as all monks have the same, no more, no less than the others. The monk then sets about spending hours in meditation and in the practice of quieting his thoughts. He is given the chore of washing the bowls and spoons after dinner, a chore he thinks is easy enough and affords him additional time to learn how to feel the enjoyment of doing his task. Every day, the monk takes his bowl and spoon, goes to the dining room with the other monks, sits in silence as he is told to do, and eats his food. He sees that his thoughts become quieter, his meditations deeper. After all, he is alone most of the time in his room. After many days of this routine, the monk, sitting at the dinner table with his bowl and spoon, glances at the bowl and spoon of the monk sitting next to him. He notices that his neighbor's bowl is shinier than his and that his neighbor's spoon appears to be carved from finer wood. Envy rises up within the monk. After dinner, the monk angrily washes the bowls and spoons, tossing them aside. Gone is his quiet life.

I understood this parable to mean that there is no escaping the unconscious: it will show itself eventually in any circumstances when the Self deems it time to begin the awakening and integration process. The parable also departs that all suffering is relative and part of the process. Soon, I began to notice the unconscious operating in those people who purported to be fully realized, and then I understood how vast and insidious the unconscious is. This process was not all about love, peace, and universal oneness, although these qualities are also important. I witnessed the dangers in the unconscious material my friends encountered in the name of a spiritual quest and how those dangers manifested in their lives. Such observations served to increase my compassion for self and for all who explore an awakening process. I began to question whether an instant transformation becomes an enduring state of consciousness, one in which the individual continues to remain in the world, connected in the world, yet free of all suffering. The problem is that such transformations do not necessarily bring lasting enlightenment, nor are they common experiences. As with many things that exist in temporality, there are cycles and uniqueness in our situations.

I was destined to be ordinary, not extraordinary. I work, come home, cook, clean, have relationships with friends, do creative projects, and enjoy time with my partner. Can a person have an awakened, conscious experience and sustain it daily while living such an ordinary life that little time is left for contemplation, prayer and meditation? Can a person be awakened consciously and be an involved person in the world, and still relate to others who are not committed to a spiritual path and invested in ending their suffering? Unlike the monk in the parable, many who begin the awakening process are not on a path that leads to a monastery where guidance, protection, and support are available. How does an ordinary person nourish and live a spiritually awakened life in the Western world?

So, I discovered it helped me not to use the term 'enlightenment,' in order not to have a predefined belief about the ultimate goal of self-realization. As I changed my spiritual approach and learned how to possess an awakened consciousness, I began to make headway toward finding stillness, compassion, an ease of life, and a release from suffering. One of the major breakthroughs I encountered was that I came to understand the relationship between suffering and pain that is not initially so obvious.

Pain versus Suffering

Life does involve pain. To hear about the death of a loved one or the loss of something important means to encounter pain. Even loving deeply can feel painful. A person would have to withdraw from and therefore block a hurtful experience in order not to endure pain.

Suffering involves being stuck within the feeling of emotional pain. A person who suffers relates a current painful moment to past events in which he / she did not release or experience the pain at that earlier time. This ego strategy of relating an immediate experience of hurt to a past situation helps that person to deal with the current circumstances by enabling him / her to feel more in control of the event and less devastated as he / she survived the previous experience. However, in truth such a process develops into unreleased or non-experienced pain in response to the current situation and eventually into a deepening of suffering.

As I personally explored the relationship between suffering and pain, I began to understand that feeling hurt is part of the human experience. Clearly, a person's suffering evolves out of the link between unreleased current pain and the pain of an earlier event. If a person has the courage and emotional fortitude to experience the pain as it is happening in the moment, then it can be done away with, and the person can move on. Therefore, in order to understand the connection between pain and suffering, I began to explore ways to release suffering and not to allow any current painful events to develop into suffering. In so doing, I kept in mind that hurtful experiences are a natural part of life, and that it is the evolved, conscious person that can experience hurt and be finished with it.

In the late 1980s, at the age of 28, I experienced a betrayal by my husband and subsequently went through a divorce. Having witnessed the destruction of my marriage and felt the depths of despair, I began to apply the theories of consciousness I had been studying both formally and informally to this life-altering event. I resolved to bring theory into practice, combining western psychology with eastern philosophies and heart-centering meditations. I learned that my crumbling marriage largely mirrored my subconscious, which had projected itself onto the screen of my relationships and marriage. By delving beneath surface behaviors and often elusive thoughts, emotions, and challenging fears, I was able to undergo consciousness transformations. These transformations changed who I was, allowing my essential being to express itself and giving me the ability to relate to situations with a still mind and from a place of clarity. Through my exploration of my own pain and suffering, I developed techniques to bring unconscious states into the light of consciousness and to maintain that awareness. By shedding light on these unconscious states, I came into a precise understanding of the many aspects of my personality. Soon, I discovered the power of acceptance and its ability to transform fearful or vulnerable aspects of my unconscious. I noticed that my ego was strengthening, not as a defensive structure but in a way that allowed the ego the openness to continue to evolve. I found the fortitude to be present with pain and allowed that feeling to take me to the depths or fullness of my experience. As I did this, I discovered that I began to take more risks in life, for I came to realize that I could be present with my fear and not allow that emotion to control me. The risks allow me to live my life more fully and to bring about the life I desire.

Dzigar Kongtrul, a Buddhist teacher (2005, p35) wrote, 'Practitioners who train in courage become true warriors. The war we wage is not with enemies outside ourselves but with the powerful forces of our own habitual tendencies and negative emotions. The greatest of these is fear. In order to become fearless, we need to experience fear.' By seeking, understanding, and becoming familiar with our deepest natures that reside unconsciously within us, we can free our inner resources so that we can step out and take on our lives in larger, more satisfying ways. In our quest to understand and *know* what it means to have a stillness of mind, then we must have larger and larger experiences with fear and other dark emotions such as despair, longing and hopelessness.

So with a new approach to my spiritual journey, I did not look toward becoming enlightened as much as I began to pay attention to who I was at unconscious levels. I started to teach myself to see my unconsciousness as it played out upon the screen of my life, as well as to incorporate compassion for these unconscious dynamics that would not only bring havoc to my life but also hold me back from living fully. Through awareness and compassionate acceptance, I began to live life more in the moment and with vibrancy and fullness.

In my work as a consciousness therapist for the last 18 years and through my personal experiences over the past 30 years, I have witnessed individuals who have used these techniques to live awakened and consciously, experiencing their lives in the present moment. I have watched as people changed their relationships with others and enhanced the quality of these personal connections. This book aims to teach these concepts and techniques, and those individuals who find a connection to this work can also undergo a remarkable transformation in their lives.

Chapter 2

Paths and Pitfalls to Enlightenment

Silence is a source of great strength.

Lao Tzu

Throughout my years of consciousness study, I have encountered many individuals who have the desire to be spiritual, more conscious, and enlightened. I have observed many such people committing time and money to achieve this goal within themselves. I have witnessed individuals making huge transformations of their belief structures and the way they were living their lives. It helps to understand that there are many paths to arriving at an awakened consciousness, as well as pitfalls along the way of a spiritual journey. I have always enjoyed a story the Swiss psychiatrist Carl Jung told about the importance of being prepared when one decides to explore his or her unconscious, a vital element in the awakening process. Jung, the founder of analytical psychology and a major contributor to the field of depth psychology, stated that if he were to encounter a large pit in the ground, which he could not go around, he would much rather have a pick, an axe, a rope, and a ladder as he approached the pit, rather than walking backwards and falling into the pit with no tools in hand (Jung, 1959). This story always puts me in touch with the importance of understanding that a spiritual journey has its hazards along the way, as well as that it requires one to have resources available when one begins to approach the unconscious and the challenges life offers.

The narratives of four of my friends who experienced 'beyond ordinary' states of consciousness and one story that hit the media at the time this book was going to print demonstrate the varied forms an awakening process can take. It is possible to see here, too, not only the benefits of living in an enlightened state but also *the importance of having inner resources and tools, of studying, of finding the quiet center within, and of being able to read the unconscious to become in direct relationship with the unconscious in order to transit the challenges safely.* What is more, in these stories the dangers and pitfalls inherent in the awakening process, which are not always openly discussed by contemporary spiritual teachers and guides, become apparent.

The Artist's Way

A friend who is an artist experiences an influx of creative energy during moments when she is painting or sculpting. A vibrating feeling buzzes through her body. Her extremities or the top of her head might tingle. At these times, her mind sort of goes away or loses its connection to our normal state of reality. She focuses intently on the paint strokes and the details of her work, and her body pulsates with energy. She experiences a transcendence of time and space. In this timeless place, hours will have gone by, and yet she thinks only minutes have passed. She describes being in this state of consciousness as involving a loss of her access to language, such as not knowing the names of objects. My friend loses a sense of a 'me or mine'. When her husband once asked where the can opener was, my friend stopped her creative process and, with paintbrush in hand, mid-stroke, stared blankly at him and slowly repeated, 'Where is the can opener?' searching her mind for the meaning of 'can opener' and just who was this person who was asking. Her husband believes she was trying to remember where the missing can opener was. If he knew that she was trying to make sense of his question, as well as figure out who he was and his importance to her, he would probably say she had finally lost her mind. This explanation is partially true, since in these moments it appears that her connection to the left-brain, where language comprehension and logical reasoning reside, is gone.

As the example of my artist friend demonstrates, the experience of this other state of consciousness can be debilitating to the ego's role of completing linear functions and simple tasks and using language and communication skills. In this aware state, it takes a great effort for a person to shift to the realm of consciousness in which he / she understands language, measures time in minutes and hours, and identifies objects. I recognize this disconnection occurs because this state of conscious awareness has not yet integrated with the left-brain, where functions such as normal linear reality reside. This phenomenon will typically emerge for people who meditate often and for long hours. After meditation, they return to left-brained functions, and the states of consciousness they have achieved in their meditations rarely become merged with their busy lives.

The ability to unite right-brained undifferentiated activity with a left-brained, logical reality state becomes easier when my friend tries to be mindful of her right brain when she is creating art. She has now begun to develop a relationship and a familiarity with this level of awareness through her artwork, learning how to incorporate this consciousness into the 'doing' areas of her life. With more understanding comes less anxiety associated with the ego's 'letting go.' When this uneasiness lessens, then a person can arrive at a state of consciousness in which time passes differently, concepts are more abstract, thoughts range from quiet to nonexistent, creativity is expanded and the ego has less control. Because of my friend's increased ability to access this state, to incorporate this state in other physical activities such as biking, running or doing housework and her lack of fear associated with it, she has begun to bring this awareness into other activities, such as visiting her difficult mother-in-law or developing intimacy in her marriage. My friend is learning to live as she paints. She is learning how to integrate her ego into this other state of consciousness. She approaches her art with awareness and with the intention of integrating this state and her ego into her everyday experience. She is beginning to recognize that this state of awareness is available and useful even when she walks away from her art and the creative process.

Danger Brings a Moment-to-Moment Consciousness State

Another friend, a rock climber, has similar transcendent experiences while leaning flat against a rock face many feet above the ground, yet she has no desire to bring this level of consciousness into her everyday life. She enters into a state of awareness in which she is focused and very much in the moment, probably due to the fact that one false move or handhold could result in a fall, or even death. Yet when she is off the mountain, an ordinary sense of awareness returns to her. She is unable to enter into this moment-to-moment, present state of being while carrying out her daily activities, activities that are, of course, not life threatening. Access to this level of consciousness only occurs when she steps onto a mountain face, when she is in relationship with the rock and when her actions could lead to harm or death. She is only able to arrive at this heightened perception by associating this state with a life-and-death situation while on the mountain face.

One may ask why she would want to access this intensified awareness as she goes about her ordinary day. Typically, she does not face life-and-death situations. She goes to work during the day and spends her evenings at home with her dogs and doing other activities. Does bringing this expanded state of awareness into daily situations generate a higher quality of experience? Perhaps, when a person has the resources to be in the moment, this consciousness state can assist him / her by bringing a fullness of heightened creativity. My rock-climbing friend could change the difficulties she has in her relations with her manager if she were able to carry this awareness into that relationship. By living in the moment, a person can experience joy while doing even the most mundane of tasks. Such pleasure can assist a person as well when he / she encounters life challenges, creative dilemmas, or a spiritual awakening process that gives rise to situations beyond his / her control. When one lives from this present state of awareness, it means one lives life without anxiety, without the constant commentary from the thoughts inside one's head. An individual can experience painful situations without going into defense against the pain and creating suffering. It is possible for a person to improve the quality of his / her life by attaining a living awareness.

A Detour into Insanity on the Road to Consciousness

Another friend, who has a very loving and gentle nature, encountered a type of awakening that can have dangerous consequences. This event happened to be not so wonderful and full of light and love. After going through a difficult divorce, she quickly found peace and comfort living in her new home, gardening, reading and meditating. Even with the meditation there continued to be a deep sense of insecurity, unworthiness and fear of what her future may have in store for her. She had sacrificed greatly for this previous marriage and its failure was burdening on her. It was not long before she had an awakening experience. The force of insight that entered her body / mind system expanded her consciousness, and its power was too great for her fragile ego to deal with or integrate. She experienced the slowing down of time, in which seconds seemed like hours, and she had no reference to space. Objects seemed to be closer to her than they actually were. She was able to notice other people's thoughts. It was as if her world and the rules she used to operate with were gone. The grasp she had on her mind was slipping. She felt as if she were in the Twilight Zone.

Even though my friend had used some meditative practices in the past, her ego had not strengthened through her previous life experiences, and she still had too many rigid ego defenses. Her self-esteem was low. She gave away her power or sacrificed herself in her relationships. Just beneath her gentle and loving nature were deep feelings of worthlessness and a deep-seated idea that she was evil—the opposite of her outward persona of gentleness. She had no preparation for an expansion of consciousness in the form of a daily practice of reflection, no prior habits of strengthening the ego through building her self-esteem or centering her mind in a practiced way.

Within a few days of this influx of energy, she began to have psychotic episodes, hallucinations, and delusions so intense that she was unable to discern reality. As an example, she experienced what she described as sexual encounters with the devil that were very real to her. In these distortions of reality, people would switch positions in their cars before her eyes, and she heard voices telling her she was a bad person and did not deserve to live.

My friend was in the midst of a spiritual emergency. Yet, she lacked any support in the community that could assist her at this level of awakening. Her awakening increased her ability to move between different states of consciousness and it was remarkable. Yet, without an established spiritual practice or a mentor, she was limited in her ability to direct her awakening process. She was spiraling into the darkness of her own unconsciousness and it was over-powering her. She was able to call her sister, who took her to an emergency room where a psychiatrist admitted her to the psychiatric hospital. He diagnosed her as schizophrenic and administered high doses of anti-psychotic medications, even though schizophrenia, along with its first psychotic outbreak, usually occurs in the late teens or early adulthood. My friend was in her 40s. The high doses of drugs quieted the voices, decreased the delusions, and assisted her in returning to 'normal.'

She had no available resources to take her through this experience differently. Since this episode, she has spent the last several years rebuilding her life, but the rape of her psyche by these intense, fearful, violent, and intrusive images that appeared real, left her unwilling to approach the awakening process again. She continues to use a tremendous amount of ego and medications to keep the darkness away. The drugs have stilled the voices and the anxieties. However, her ego puts forth effort to be in control of everything in her environment and keeps up a running commentary within her mind in order to dispel any quiet. For my friend, a mind that is at peace provides the space for her to tap into this powerful influx of energy, and she is not prepared to do that at this time.

I Am Enlightened and You Are Not

Oftentimes, people who proclaim themselves enlightened act in ways that are not in alignment with their teachings or in how they live their lives. Seduction exists on the spiritual path just as it does in the ordinary, material world, and it can be a large obstacle. From a material perspective, we witness advertising for new cars, beautiful homes, and new gadgets, things that we want to possess and that we want now because we see ourselves as lacking. The fear that surrounds our feeling that we are deficient allows us to make decisions that result in financial bankruptcy, or else we might obtain an object only to find that it does not fulfill its promise to make us happier. The same holds true in the spiritual world, except the fear is not about a material but rather a spiritual lack.

If we believe that someone else has more spiritual currency then we do and that they are therefore better than we are, we have set ourselves up to be seduced. This occurs quite often with people who are on a quest for self-understanding, harmony, love, compassion, wisdom, spiritual awakening or even power. Seduction, while it arises out of fear, is one of the more difficult states of awareness to become conscious of and to understand in one, as it feels good and provides a solution to the underlying fear. In this case, the hidden anxiety could be the hierarchical system we have just created within our mind regarding spirituality and the desire to be high on that spiritual ladder in order to feel safe, good enough that our external world would reflect riches as some sort of reward for our goodness, or for some other hidden reason. The enticement of spirituality then becomes a major barrier in self-realization or in the awakening process.

As this book was going to print, a story hit the media in which tragic events occurred at a sweat lodge ceremony in Arizona resulting in the deaths of three people and the hospitalization of approximately 20 others. The man who was leading the lodge had built a very successful career as a motivational speaker whose life philosophy he discussed in his books as 'You can have all you desire by changing your beliefs and thoughts bringing them into alignment with your desires.' This philosophy while powerful and life changing to some people, does not hold importance or interest to the deep psyche, the spiritual feminine or other states of consciousness that are not ego-based.

Sweat Lodges are an important Native American ritual, led by experienced Lodge Keepers, who are typically Native American people descended from Native American shamans, or have been trained by a Native American experienced elder or leader. In the sweat I have attended the Lodge Keeper was a Native American Sioux whose father, grandfather and great-grandfather were shamans of his tribe. His initiations into the deeper realms of consciousness included rites of passage such as the Sundance ritual involving the piercing of the fleshy parts of his breast, inserting hooks and being strung up from a tree for a pre-determined amount of time. The scars on his body were indications of his commitment to his legacy and the completion of these rites of passages he had undergone to earn his rightful place as a shaman to his people.

These initiations prepared the shaman giving him / her the ability to enter these deeper states of consciousness, as well as obtain the ability to enter collective forces for the members of his / her tribe. The shaman, trained in accessing non-ordinary states of mind, understands that he / she must have humility or deep respect for the Great Spirit or these unconscious forces. This means the surface ego cannot be involved in these forces as it will either fall into seduction through intoxication or be rendered helpless through victimizing energies. To enter into such rituals or deep states of awareness that does not honor the depths and power of the feminine energies or is entered from a place of surface ego directed consciousness, such as material or enhancing one's ego, is flirting with disaster both physically and mentally. For the ways of manifesting from these states of consciousness do not operate from the same rules or guidelines as an ego-directed conscious states.

The man leading the sweat in Arizona appeared not to have much experience of these other states of consciousness and the dangers that could occur. Therefore, he was unprepared to handle the events that led to the deaths of these people and the aftermath. I have witnessed in my practice people who are not experienced in the arts of meditation or accessing states of consciousness unfamiliar to their egos having panic attacks or increased life challenges. One sensitive young woman I know now suffers from panic after attending an ashram in India. Another group of spiritual individuals wanted to take their methods of accelerating spiritually to teenage participants. Soon after this practice, several of these teenage participants committed suicide. The group relocated their operations to another state to avoid the effects of negative press to their organization. The members of this group, involved with the dogma of their teachings, did not have the knowledge or under-standing of the importance of strong ego growth that typically does not occur before the age of 18. This ego strength is important as a basis for moving one's mind into the deeper states of consciousness. I think this is important in understanding the dangers of the depths of feminine and respecting this. Finding a mentor or practitioner well versed, educated, and credentialed in these practices is an essential task before starting depth work and self-exploration. I mean, would you climb Mount Everest without training and having an experienced guide?

The Danger of Spiritual Seduction

One of my friends became the close personal assistant to a self-proclaimed, enlightened female guru who had attracted a large group of followers in several countries. My friend desired to become enlightened, as was evident in his commitment and personal sacrifices. He surrendered his money and other posses-sions to the guru's organization, as the group taught a lesson of nonattachment to the material world.

However, the organization's practice of acquiring the properties and monies of their new followers, in order to break a person's attachment to the material world seemed to me inher-ently contradictory. One of the purposes of the group appeared to be exploiting the wealth of its new members. The leadership's single-minded pursuit of these well-to-do patrons who sought their services also belied a possible interior motive in the guise of spirituality. The focus on acquiring new members required the group to assess a person's financial status or ability to bring in revenue. It also provided the guru with financial security and her own accumulation of wealth.

When individuals awaken and can incorporate a practice of understanding their unconscious dynamics, and when those dynamics may play out, then they provide less of a hook that allows others to manipulate them. My friend's desire to be part of this group that proclaimed to know the way to enlightenment was too much for him to set aside. He became deeply attached to this organization, wanting the guru to lead him into a higher state of awareness. The group was able to seduce him due to his fear that he would never find what he was searching for without their guidance and teaching. At the root of seduction is fear and when we recognize that fear is operating within us we need to be cautious in the actions that arise from this state. In truth, as upcoming chapters on awareness and power and control will show, relationships in and of themselves can become one's most profound teacher and a tool for fully manifesting in temporal reality.

The organization's guru would closet herself away from anyone other than her closest devotees, claiming that this practice maintained the level of vibration and energy flow through her body that served to initiate others into their awakening process as well as propel them into a state of unconditional love. She would exert control over her devotees from this isolated position, telling them whom they would marry, where they would live, and when they would leave their families. Many of her teachings contained truths and were in the form of the Eastern philosophies that continue to gain popularity in the West. These modes of thought are derived from the Tao and Buddhism, and they also included tenets of Christianity. The strongest messages that the group's members repeated over and over in a singsong cadence were, 'The time has come for you to end your suffering,' 'You do not want to enter into another cycle of suffering again and again,' 'Time has run out,' and 'The time is now.' These statements are based in fear, and they play upon an individual's insecurities. These messages fly in direct opposition to understanding the mystery of the transcendental nature of temporality and manifestation. Maybe it is not about trying to get out of here but how to live the mystery more fully, honoring life's richness, and becoming as conscious if and when possible.

This organization's attraction is their ability to bring a person into an ecstatic state of unconditional love. I witnessed many followers having rewarding spiritual experiences. The group offered people a lot, leading them through consciousness breakthroughs and helping them to discard old belief systems that did not serve them well. Many members had 'breakthroughs' in which they vibrated with life-force energy. Their eyes would sparkle, and oftentimes they felt a love for everything and everyone. They had achieved unity with the world. Their joy was beautiful, and I longed to experience it. My encounter with this group through knowing my friend occurred in the early 1990s, during a time when spiritual group encounters were on the rise. I believed that this organization had found an answer to the fast-track enlightenment craze that was permeating the Western world.

Of course, I was attracted to the message, as I wanted to be happy and to end my own despair and the suffering that accompanied it. This group could easily become an escape from my own challenging of my fears. It took a great effort on my part not to allow the group and my friend to seduce me by their teachings. Their instruction, I realized, fed my attachment to escaping from a world of suffering. I, too, wanted to throw caution aside and join the group. My concept of enlightenment at this time played into my ego's illusion that I could reach a state of happiness and bliss by trading the strife and struggle of the material world for the illusion of protectiveness and safety the guru offered.

Many teachers allude to this concept of a higher consciousness, asserting that people can reach enlightenment by buying into their type of spiritual practice. However, as discussed in Chapter 1, this form of perfected awareness is actually beyond the control of the individual, and its pursuit is usually ego-driven as an escape from suffering. Spiritual realization cannot be obtained based on this motivation. A friend and I have discussed how many of the spiritual teachers with whom we have come into contact talk about their own journey to a more enlightened place. These teachers seem to regard themselves as having something, such as a knowledge, that others do not, thus creating a separation between themselves and other individuals and thereby undermining the teachers' status as the 'enlightened'. Once this separation occurs and there is no awareness, then these teachers have just stepped out of their enlightened state. Such spiritual guides are actually expressing unconsciousness within themselves through their separation from others, as I witnessed in the group mentioned above.

Fortunately, I had enough discernment at this time to recognize the seduction that this cult existence had over me. I had developed enough ability to understand that the guru's control over her followers oftentimes inflicted suffering upon other people not involved in the group. Women left their children to serve the collective, and husbands and wives had multiple affairs, all in the name of freeing themselves of ego attachments, a popular belief in Eastern philosophy. Furthermore, the guru guided and approved of these activities. I had difficulty accepting the tenets of the group's message of ending personal suffering when the very actions of those who claimed to be enlightened caused suffering in others.

Having witnessed these followers' actions, I understood that they were actually in many ways not living in an awakened state, yet most of them were proclaiming enlightenment. They were unaware of their unconscious material and unable to discern how their unconsciousness was affecting other people around them. For example, some participants would say that the pain caused to their partners by their sexual freedom was due to their partners not being as 'realized' as they were.

I was interested in how people could have a higher vibration of energy coursing through their bodies, a state they professed was an indication of their heightened awareness, and yet have large unconscious dynamics that continued to function within their relationships. Their intense energy level would last a day or even a few weeks after their group meetings, but these people did not appear to have integrated it into a conscious living experience. The desire and commitment of these followers to become more aware was soundly proven by their personal sacri-fices. However, I had a sense that underneath their desires lay the fear that was inherent in the organization's message, 'You are doomed if you do not break through rigid thought patterns, and you need to do that now. Enlightenment is only achieved within this group.' There was not an honored recognition of the people who live an unawakened and unconscious life and the purpose this serves the collective. Consciousness transformations do not always require conscious participation only an acceptance for what is and experiencing the fullness of the situation may be all that is necessary.

I recently encountered my friend who has spent 12 years in this group, intensely focused on enlightenment. He appeared drawn, tired, and weary from his quest. The light that was in his eyes a few years ago was now gone. He did regard himself as enlightened, and he had a great deal of insight. He informed me that he had transformed his unconscious patterns. Yet he continued to follow without question, although against his better judgment, the commands of his guru, which was one of his patterns that contributed to his suffering. This pattern appeared to be operating, however, on an unconscious level in regards to this guru, and he was unwilling or unable to perceive it. In order to become aware of this pattern, he would need to risk finding spiritual enlightenment on his own or to live without the safety his guru provided. The guru continued to dictate with whom he was to be in relationship and where he was to live. Because he was unwilling to face the consequences that joining this group had had on his life and the bargain he had made to become enlightened, this large pattern was draining his vital energy. Challenging his underlying fears would allow him to realize the purpose of his current situation which may be his experience of being in service to the larger feminine whether it was reflected with the female guru or the organization. To come into that understanding may provide the peace and compassion that he has sacrificed so much to obtain.

While I honored the path that he was on and felt compassion

for the sacrifices he had made toward his spiritual growth, as well as all that I had given up in my own life, I felt relieved I had escaped this one. I was grateful that many years earlier I had had enough discernment to choose to follow my own direction in spite of the great seductive power of this collective. I believe that the practices I talk about in this book allowed me to be aware of my own unconscious dynamics, enough to avoid this 'pitfall', and to not need to explore this event in my life, as I was to delve into other experiences that involved awakening. Many of those experiences I am sure my friend is sighing and repeating to himself, 'Wow, I am glad I didn't have to live that experience.'

Going It Alone

I desired and was committed to achieving a state of consciousness that felt more sustained across time, and that did not depend on a group consciousness to arrive at a temporary state within myself. I wanted my awareness to be supported within my own self, independent from a collective, although I might draw on a collective to deepen my own process. I did not want enlightenment to mean that I must isolate myself from humanity. I aimed for a level of consciousness that could thrive in the darkness that existed in our world and could be in relationship with the ever-changing dynamic of life. I sought to have a living connection with the unconscious. I wanted to free my mind from the limitations and fear-driven motivations that seemed to underlie most of my actions. This link to my inner self would provide me with the ability to shine a light onto the darkness of my unconscious material to become a partner to whatever life offered up for me. I wanted to be a dance partner with my life's situations and not perceive my life situations as the song of the dance. Again, the experience of having a living connection sparked in me the desire to develop the tools and resources to sustain this state of conscious living. I would encounter spiritual collectives, teachers, guides, life situations, and other people that assisted me in reaching this goal, as well as undertake formal education to learn as much as I could about the unconscious mind.

The German author Herman Hesse writes about a situation similar to that of my friend and I who took two different paths to spiritual realization in his novel *Siddhartha* (Hesse, 1961). Siddhartha and his best friend, Govinda, are spiritual seekers, born into the Brahmin tradition, and as adults, they join the Samanas. Siddhartha recognizes that the spiritual teachers he meets among the Samanas appear to have missing at their inner core a direct experience of enlightenment. Thus, Siddhartha becomes disillusioned with their teachings. Being of a more independent mind, he leaves the Samanas to pursue enlightenment by being in the world, while his friend Govinda, shocked at Siddhartha's decision, decides to remain. He instead chooses the monk's life in his attempt to reach enlightenment

Many years later, the two friend's paths cross, and it is each man's willingness to experience the other at a depth of relationship that provides a means for them to reach their life-long search for enlightenment. At the time of their meeting, Siddhartha has achieved enlightenment by working alongside an enlightened ferry driver, something he was unable to find from previous spiritual teachers he had met on his journey. His transformational process involved little consciousness participation, only being present and fully taking in his experience with the ferry driver. Siddhartha has no need to enlighten his friend, as his own attachment to being enlightened no longer exists and he holds no judgment of others. Govinda, recognizing Siddhartha's state of awareness, suddenly finds acceptance for his own un-enlightened state and all aspects within himself that he also becomes enlightened in that moment. The outcome of their meeting signifies that both men have encountered enlightenment. No path is the right path, and no teaching the only teaching. Only desire, commitment and courage is the common element. It is important to realize that each person's path is the suitable one for that person—whether he / she is seeking spiritual realization or living an unconscious existence.

Living the Aspects of My Unlived Life

The story of Siddhartha demonstrates to me that a variety of avenues, different teachings, community with others, full experience of one's life events, and relationships with all types of people can bring a person into an awakening experience. The experiences of my friends, family, acquaintances, clients, and patients whom I treat in the Emergency Room have shown me the importance they have in my personal consciousness evolution. It is as if in each encounter or interaction I have with someone, that person is living out some part of my unlived reality of an unchosen life. It seems to me that at some deciding point in my own life, the path I did not choose, a deep fear I did not see, or a potential I had not realized becomes an experience of a person with whom I later cross paths in my life. Through my involvement with this person, I also come into touch with that unlived or unseen part within myself.

This is a notion that is quite similar to parallel universes. Quantum scientists maintain that at every choice point in an individual's life, that potential life splits off into another universe to live out that decision (Vicente, 2004). The friend who forfeited herself for children, husband, and family; the friend driven to insanity during her awakening experience; the friend who sacrificed his self for preconceived ideas of enlightenment; the friend who achieved critical acclaim for her academic work; the homeless man who expresses his despair and fear of total helplessness that he might not be able to live on the streets; the friend who lives simply and happily without the entrapments of societal expectations; the businessman who feels suicidal and hopeless because he is in financial and professional ruin; the friend who sells herself into a wealthy, loveless marriage for security and societal approval; the friend who is dealing with breast cancer and the dismemberment of her body—all express some aspect of my life that at some decision point became an unlived expression of my Self. Becoming aware that each person I encounter holds some aspect within my conscious and unconscious self, then I can see my relationship to this person reflects back to me how far along I am on the path of awakening. The more awakened I am, the more compassion I have in my relationships with others' suffering and experiences.

My witnessing these experiences of my friends stimulated my questioning and interest in learning more about our states of consciousness—in particular, how to develop a present and enduring state of inner awareness along with compassionate understanding. Throughout many years of formal and informal study, I recognized that being aware in the moment was not a once-and-forever experience. In my case, there appeared to be progressive increments of consciousness toward a final step of integration of a particular dynamic or ego structure that had once operated as defense. These patterns or defenses appear to occur in cycles just as life appears in cycles. Then, I would enter this cycle that reflected a certain pattern again maybe with less stress or anxiety associated with the pattern. Then I would proceed on to the next dynamic or ego structure that was beckoning to me to go into a depth of understanding. As I became aware of the structure, I would recognize and remain present with the associated emotion or suffering, until something occurred that finally released and integrated the structure into a state of stillness. The more I continued to work with this process, the less and less reactive I became to situations. The less reactive I became, the more the quality of my experience was heightened. The pattern may or may not go away but my relationship with the pattern would change, so that it didn't matter if the pattern continued to exist in my life. I realized I did not have control over these patterns manifesting or not in my experiences, the Self partly orchestrates this. But, I did have control over the quality of my experience once I had awakened to it. It takes an ability of concentration and focus that can be honed with meditative practices.

My curiosity served to fuel my desire to bring a state of conscious presence or a profound awareness into my ordinary, day-to-day experience. As I witnessed the insidious nature of the unconscious, I continued to develop tools that would help not only me but also other individuals to perceive our unconsciousness, increase our awareness, and provide resources that would become invaluable when we encounter those pitfalls along the way.

I began to formulate a method of centering that involved seating the awareness, or the mind's eye in the center of the chest, the heart-center. This practice, as I would find out years later, automatically places a person's awareness into the observer state of consciousness that allows that person to maintain a concentrated focus and being present in the moment more easily. This tool of heart centered practice can be found on my web page and is highly recommended as a practice before delving into the exercises provided in this book. Another tool I developed was a way to release suffering from my consciousness and to allow myself to experience pain without it transforming into suffering. A third tool speaks to how we relate to objects, people, and situations, and how we regard these relationships as a way to make us aware and to help us understand our unconscious material. These strategies enhanced my ability to read the unconscious and become present in the moment.

As we explore our unconscious natures, the depths of that darkness can manifest into our external realities in dangerous forms or experiences. Having these tools can assist us in bringing forth the appropriate action necessary for any situation that arises. When we have awareness along with compassion and the understanding that other people may carry our own deep darkness, then we can recognize their sacrifice for our growth opportunity. The people that we meet and that carry our dark structures provide an opportunity for us to experience this darkness without taking it on in our own body and mind system.

By 1994, other than having brief moments of awareness throughout my day and my initial awakening process, I typically could reach this present state of awareness in meditation, in my therapy sessions with clients, or when alone and quiet. That is, until one fateful evening at a summer lake resort, when I had a major encounter, an earth-shaking one that brought me face-to-face with my deepest fear, the threat of physical death.

Chapter 3

Introduction to Integrative Consciousness

To a mind that is still the whole universe surrenders.

Chuang Tzu

My Desire Realized: An Experience with Conscious Presence

Scary Ed McPerry was an infamous, notorious man who resided near the area's largest lake resort, where I spent my summer weekends as a young adult enjoying the water, sun, and my friends. Ed was known for his stunts that were either the result of stupidity or full-throttle, dangerous risk-taking. It is interesting how life will put you in contact with an extreme individual that you may never have an opportunity in your normal day-to-day life to encounter. It is even more interesting to note that an experience with this type of individual could also contain a profound moment in your awakening process.

As an example of the dangerousness of this man, legend had it that Ed once took his jet ski out on the lake and was following his friends while they were waterskiing. One young man, on waterskis, dropped the ski rope, slowly lowered himself into the lake, and was treading water until his friends returned to pick him up. Ed, who had been trailing too closely on the jet ski, could not maneuver around his friend and was unable to avoid hitting him. To hear Ed tell the story, he had gotten 'air' off of the man's face. As the jet ski lifted out of the water, Ed had a momentary glance at the horrified, shocked look on the face of the skier, who, fortunately, came out of the incident unscathed. Ed, still on the jet ski, flew several feet into the air before landing in the back of the moving ski boat. A combination of these types of daring feats warranted Ed to inscribe on his jet ski his moniker, 'Scary Ed McPerry,' and everyone who knew of him at the lake thought the nickname was fitting.

So here it was, the end of Ed's eventful, drama-filled summer at the lake, which was so unlike my peaceful, meditative, and being-with-nature, summer experience. Yet, these two different worlds merged and I soon found myself crossing paths with Ed.

This was the summer that I set the intention to explore how to bring an awareness of the present moment into living consciousness. I was about to have that experience. I assumed it would come in the classroom or a consciousness seminar, as I had just enrolled in a university to pursue my doctorate on the study of consciousness. But life, in its infinite wisdom, had something else in store, a much more direct and emphatic way of bringing that experience to me.

It was dusk, and people were taking their boats off the lake for the night. As I walked along the street by a donut shop in the lake village, I suddenly felt something like a metal rod poking in my back, and I was being pushed into a small boathouse along with an older woman. Once inside, I was shoved forward. I turned and was looking down a long-barreled shotgun into the contorted face of Scary Ed. Underneath a Chicago Cubs baseball cap, his eyes were large and bugged out, darting back and forth from me to the other woman. He looked like Nicholas Cage in the movie 'The Face Off'—a crazed, deranged look of not being able to connect emotionally, morally, or in any other way to another individual or even with this reality.

By his erratic behavior and the quick, jerky motions of the gun, I knew he was on some kind of drug, which I later discovered was crack. I understood that when the infamous, unpredictable Ed was on crack, he became a dangerous person. He was ranting and raving about something, and as far as I was concerned, he could have been speaking a foreign language. I was unable to comprehend his words, perhaps due to my own mind freezing up in complete terror. The older woman standing beside me shook violently and moaned quietly. From the corner of my eye, I saw her sink to her knees. Ed pointed the gun first in her direction and then in mine, and I knew her behavior was irritating him. An incomprehensible thought came to me: he probably will shoot her first, hopefully miss, and then maybe I will have time to try to get all three of us out of this situation alive.

The thought allowed me to come out of my frozen-mind state, and I saw that at least my demeanor was not drawing his attention or anger. The image of a bullet entering my head and my brains exiting out the back kept flashing through my mind. I was terrified, but at least I did not panic. The only words I could muster were, 'Ed, please put the gun down. You don't want to be doing this.' I motioned repeatedly with my hands, palms down, to emphasize putting the gun down. I was too afraid to say or do anything else for fear that my actions would cause Ed to pull that trigger, turning into reality the image of a bullet passing through my head.

Then, something happened that I had only read about from enlightened teachers and had only experienced in meditation, and that I certainly did not expect would occur when a man was pointing a gun to my head. I felt as if there was an actual physical snap within my brain, and my awareness dropped to my heart-center, the place where I had practiced seating my mind over many years of meditation while 'sitting' with the fears of my ego. This seating of my mind always automatically places me in the 'witness state' of being. I register with slight amazement my centered state. This time, however, this state of consciousness differed from my meditative state, as my consciousness was front and center, while my ego was still ruminating in the background, rendered helpless by the image of my head being blown off. This centered state was acting on the physical world, not passive in meditation. I continued to repeat, 'Ed, please put the gun down. You don't want to be doing this.'

An incredible stillness came over me, independent of my fear of dying. This composure differed from a meditative calmness and peace. It was more substantial and real, arrived at in a living, creative experience with these people. I was focused and very much aware of my moment-to-moment interactions with this man, as well as the sobbing woman at my side. Even though Ed had a gun, I had no sense that he was the one in control or that he had power over me, or I over him. We both were dancing a surreal dance of life, each moving in relationship to one another. I had no anger or judgment toward this man who held me against my will and at gunpoint. I felt a deep sense of compassion for his suffering, and I thought of his utter powerlessness to control events in his life, a powerlessness that had driven him to this point.

He moved his aim from me to the other woman, knocking off the baseball cap that was sitting precariously on his head. Then, I did something that the S.W.A.T. team later told me was the wrong thing to do if I wanted to live through such an experience. I slowly walked toward Ed and the shotgun. My ego had been running its commentary: 'I can't believe you are doing this, you fool! You are going to get yourself shot!' But from my state of serenity, with my first step, my ego began to calm down. I knew that if Ed pulled the trigger, this state of stillness would support me through the next moment, even if it meant entering through the portal of death.

When I came within a few inches of the barrel, I stepped aside and bent over, picked up the baseball cap that had fallen to the floor, and placed it on Ed's head. I put my hand on his arm and said for the last time, 'Ed, you don't want to be doing this.' Then, unbelievably, I walked back in front of the gun with the barrel just inches from my chest. A minute later, Ed left the building, firing off three or four shots into the dusky, evening sky.

Later, I understood why the S.W.A.T. team, whose members

are trained to deal with power-and-control situations and to work within those dynamics, told me that if a person walks toward a man with a gun pointed at him / her, it is a sign of aggression, and that the man will usually shoot. However, I realized that the state of consciousness I had accessed had allowed me to step out of the power dynamics in this situation. I had had no awareness that Ed possessed any power over me, even though he had held the gun. I had released the attachment of avoiding death, Ed's one source of power over me. I also did not have a desire to have any power over Ed, only a sense of compassion for his state of powerlessness and the events in his life that had driven him to this point. I had recognized that if I were not operating out of customary structures of power and control, then Ed would not be able to relate to me from the power arena. That is why, I believe, he left the boathouse seconds later.

Suffering No More

The next day, I was surprised when a Victim's Advocate contacted me. I could not comprehend myself as a victim. The woman from this organization told me, 'I am confused. I want to meet the woman that went through this hostage experience.' I was that woman, I told her. She said that I did not seem like the people she had worked with who had undergone such trauma in their lives, that I was not demonstrating any acute traumatic symptoms. She wanted to know why. She said that for me to talk about it with such calmness that was not detached was as though many years had gone by since the traumatic event, not as if it had happened only the night before. She was right. I had experienced no post-traumatic symptoms from this event. In fact, I had slept like a baby that night as well as subsequent nights.

Based on this observation, I understood that when an experience occurs in a present state of consciousness, then the experience itself becomes absorbed into this larger state of consciousness. The experience is not acted upon by a defended ego state. I had gone through a painful situation—the real threat of my life ending—allowed my vulnerability to powerlessness to occur, integrated it within the moment, and therefore it did not become a suffering pattern within my ego. I was able to experience the process that I had begun to study and understand from many years of practice regarding how to achieve an enduring state of consciousness. A person can have the ability to experience pain or suffering when encountering a conflictual moment, even if the moment is a traumatic event.

I also understood later that evening that Ed carried my fear of being rendered powerless in life. I had this insight during the experience with Ed. I recognized that my fear of powerlessness was at this same level, a level where I could reach for power with another human being and threaten him / her due to my own feelings of powerlessness. I also realized that when we go through a consciousness transformation, the ego experiences no control or is rendered powerless. The outer experience reflects the inner process the ego encounters with transformation. My ability to find acceptance of Ed's powerlessness and how it motivated him to go so far as to hold two people at gunpoint was related to my ability to find acceptance of my own levels of powerlessness.

A year later, Ed was out of prison and knocking on my door. Reflecting back, I often wonder why I opened the door, but at the time I sensed no danger. He told me he wanted to thank me because something had happened during that episode that had changed the direction of what he had planned. He said he would have shot both the woman and me, but that in the course of my interaction with him he had decided to leave. He appeared puzzled and was waiting for an explanation from me. It did not occur to me to explore this further with him. I told him that something had happened that was profound. He did understand that due to his altering the course of what he had planned, he was consequently not spending his life in prison and two women

44

lived to see another day.

Absorption of Ego

· My encounter with Ed increased my ability to live from a conscious, centered, and present state of awareness. I developed a daily spiritual practice that issued from a living experience of the moment in which I could see my unconscious and conscious dynamics as they manifested in my reality. In other words, I could live life without the analysis and study ordinarily required to reach this enduring state of consciousness. My practice became more and more in the moment as I went about my day, as opposed to spending hours and hours daily in study and meditation. I wished to clarify my experience and start to teach this practice to my clients. Would I be able to assist them in their 'A-ha' moments through a more relaxed, yet formalized way of approaching consciousness, in other words, a day-to-day relationship with the unconscious and its unfolding?

When I had encountered Ed, I had felt grounded in this state of conscious awareness of the here and now. By this, I mean I focused my mind. It was different from the state of consciousness that I enter in meditation. There was fullness to this state, possibly because I was attending to the moment, creating from this awareness into physical reality. I knew that from this expanded state of consciousness, I could operate in the physical world, make decisions, and have the desire to carry through with those decisions without anxiety behind my actions. I could see my motivations and be aware of my relationships in the moment as an event played out. I was 'co-creating' with my experience. I had been co-creating with Ed, the other woman, and myself. That is, as I acted, and he acted, and she acted, we shaped a moment and moved toward the outcome of our joint experience.

In those times in adulthood when the unconscious, fate, or an objective circumstance confronts the ego with defeat—or in my case, possible death—lie the opportunities for the most important psychological developments to occur. This appears to be because in facing actual physical death or even a profound defeat, the ego surrenders its need to control, becomes subservient to another process that can move with the situation differently and from resources the ego does not have access to. It takes a maximum level of despair, helplessness and then vulnerability as a prerequisite for transformation. Once that final defense is down, then integration *may* occur. For the Soul is not interested in survival, it is interested in engaging the living experience and process itself. In my case, when I confronted what appeared to be imminent death, I moved into a state of consciousness that I had typically practiced in meditations while sitting with my worst fears, fears that I became aware of by seeing my unconsciousness as it was projected onto the screen of my life. This state of consciousness provided me the resource to witness and co-create my experience.

I understood that the moment in which we are living carries the fullness of life and all of its possibilities to co-create. I wondered, could this state of consciousness be sustained throughout the day in a more consistent manner without requiring a crisis to bring it on? If I was able to obtain such awareness while facing possible death, then could I sustain consciousness daily in a chaotic world? I was not living in a monastery or secluding myself in a room without any human contact. I was actually leading my life doing what I love to do, that is, attending to those who suffer mentally and emotionally and having a life with my family and friends. From that point on, I devoted my practice to developing a structure for myself that allowed me to realize this goal of an enduring, conscious, and awakened state.

Having seen the difficulty my friend in the cult had in relating to the physical world while maintaining an enduring state of awakened consciousness, I realized the difficulty that exists when a person cannot see his / her unconscious patterning, or ego defenses, as they continue to play out, sometimes in ways that are quite dramatic. The ability to become aware of unconscious material, as it surfaces, is an integral step in sustaining an awakened level of awareness that ultimately leads to an enduring state of consciousness.

The experience I had in the boathouse with Ed gave me an insight about the valuable role ego plays in integrating spirit into the body and manifesting consciousness through experience. I saw ego in a new light, one in which the ego is initially valuable in helping a person to develop a sense of self and ego strength, especially during our early adult life. Then, perhaps as a person moves into a later stage of development, ego, seated in its strength, stays present with vulnerability to the fear and without building ego-defense. Typically, when a person feels fear, the ego defends through mechanisms of rationalizations, denials, and projections, to name a few. An undefended ego, however, allows itself to be absorbed by this state of heightened consciousness. This absorption process integrates ego with a heightened perceptual conscious state. The result of this integration is then the ability to be present and aware in situations without inter-jecting ego defense onto the situation.

Observation of Ego Defense Operating

To take a simple example of ego defense, let's say you approach a grocery line and notice that it is long. You become angry at the wait. In this moment, anger represents a fear-based perception of the unconscious that can be the result of a variety of reasons. You may observe that your wait is due to the slowness and inexpe-rience of your cashier. Your relationship with inexperience as your projection onto the cashier may represent your own fear of insecurity when you are in situations where you are inexperi-enced. Another example may be, as you wait in line, you begin to feel unattended to. This lack of attention brings up feelings of rejection, worthlessness, and so forth. If you can be aware that this projection of insecurity or worthlessness onto the cashier represents your own emotions and your relationship of self, then the process begins of allowing the ego to take back and recognize the projection. Awareness is more than insight or an intellectual understanding, it also incorporates recognizing the emotion associated with the experience. So, awareness became my first component in obtaining integrative consciousness.

A second component that supports the integrative consciousness process is an open heart of compassion and unconditional love, which allows acceptance, especially acceptance of vulnerability to the situation or the person that one encounters. Acceptance allows the ego to drop its defensive structure. Using our above example, you would have the awareness that your fear of inexperience makes you feel insecure. By your allowing the complete acceptance of this fear, then the ego would be able to fully take back its defensive structure that it is projecting onto the cashier and the shadow becomes integrated into the larger state of being or Self. You would no longer feel angry at the wait because you would not be projecting the fear of inexperience onto the situation. As a result, you would feel patient. If you have awareness, acceptance, and integration, then you experience a state of consciousness that has an integrated ego state or *being*. You have as well a heightened awareness that results in an enduring, grounded state of consciousness, and that leads to a deep stillness of the mind and a truly compassionate approach to life. This is my definition of conscious awakening.

Through the vicarious experiences of my friends and my own life encounters, I also observed the intense fear associated with the ego's surrender into that larger state of consciousness. The ego greatly fears giving up control, power and being annihilated. These fearful patterns exist both consciously and unconsciously and begin to manifest in our physical reality, usually as control dynamics, beckoning us to challenge the illusions they represent.

If we are aware and can see these control dynamics, then we can work with them until the dynamics release, or, more precisely, until the ego dynamic is absorbed into the larger state of consciousness or the Self. The more we release, then, the more present in the moment we become, the quieter of mind.

What Is Stillness?

Stillness is a quiet mind. Thought continues to exist, but we experience fewer and fewer conflicted thoughts. Within the still mind, there is no anxiety or fear behind the thought. A thought comes in, we attend to it, and then it leaves. Some spiritual teachers view stillness as the space between each thought. As a result of our observing the space between thoughts, say, an observation that is obtained through meditation, the thoughts come less frequently into our mind. This process is due to the focus on stillness. The more still we are, the more present in the moment we become; the more present we are, the more still our mind. Only once we are able to slow our mind can we really attend to the present moment.

The key to stillness is, first, to have ego strength and awareness, which is the ability to catch or see the unconscious and allow it to be conscious, and secondly, to possess a depth of compassionate acceptance. Compassionate acceptance is the willingness to experience the suchness of the event, taking it in, experiencing it as completely and fully as possible. This compassionate awareness is not always constant, as there are at all times aspects on a personal egoic level that are not yet evolved enough to contain the larger conscious perspective. These two components (awareness and acceptance) result in the third component, integrative consciousness, an enduring state of conscious, compassionate awareness. Personal work accompanies an awakening process and increases the ability to sustain a more fully conscious life. My previous expectations of what enlightenment was did not allow me to appreciate my unique path, or the many different ways others have of achieving an 'enlightened' and self-realized life, or even to appreciate the individual who lives an unconscious experience.

Awareness, Acceptance, and Integration

I have since understood that the path to enlightenment or self-realization is not necessarily an all-or-nothing, instant, transformational event, but rather that it occurs in a series of cycles or stages. I realize now that to be enlightened is, first, about desiring and committing to the process. Second, it is about having those two components of awareness, and acceptance that contains a dimension of a vulnerable and compassionate quality of relationship to experience. Third, it is about integrating the undefended ego structure into the larger state of consciousness.

A fourth component of the awakening process, which I will discuss later, is an element that naturally evolves—providing conscious service to the community. This factor entails having the ability to hold one's own or another's suffering in a space of compassion despite the fear of allowing that suffering in. This piece is missing in many people who are looked upon as enlightened.

As I developed my own approach to consciousness transformation, I examined the psychological processes that appear to underlie the state of awakened consciousness—as defined, in part, by psychological and consciousness theorists such as Carl Jung, A. H. Almass, and Brugh Joy—and redefined this phenomenon as 'Integrative Consciousness'. Integrative Consciousness is a process of becoming conscious and aware, experiencing the realness and fullness of who you are in the present moment, and being open to acceptance and the emotional quality of compassion in an experience, which ultimately results in the ego structure being absorbed into an expanded, enduring state of consciousness. The ego matures in its development and the expanded consciousness contains a new quality of fullness and substance.

The following chapters provide the tools and resources I have found invaluable in the process of awakening to consciousness and evolving toward Integrative Consciousness. I provide actual experiences from my life, as well as examples that represent the experiences of others I have encountered on this journey. But first, the next chapter discusses the factors that come into play when a person begins to make that leap into consciousness awakening.

Exercise

1. The aim is to have an experience of being in the present moment state of consciousness. Typically, the experience of awe and wonderment brings in the state of being present in the moment, although not an enduring state of consciousness.

    Look at an object in nature: a flower, the mountains, the ocean, etc. Observe the object without labeling or naming it with thought. Try to hold and experience the object without running any commentary within your mind. See if you can experience the wonderment of the object. If you are able to achieve this, then you are in the state of consciousness that is described as being present in the moment.

2. Try to notice a time when you are involved in a repetitive or tedious act, and allow yourself to attend to the act. Pay attention to how, before, you might have been on autopilot, the mind drifting off with all different thoughts. You might have had thoughts of a future or a past event. You were not present in the moment with the act.

    Now, try to stay in the moment, observing what is occurring in front of you. Observe your thoughts. Do your thoughts initially reflect large, stressful situations in your life? As you begin to turn your attention to your thoughts, does the content become less and less fear based?

The awareness you are experiencing is becoming more present in the moment. Observe how this awareness has an effect on anxiety as it is expressed in rumination on stressful thoughts and situations. Do these thoughts become less and less frequent?

Chapter 4

The Beginning

'Neo, sooner or later you're going to realize just as I did that there's a difference between knowing the path and walking the path.'
Morpheus, The Matrix

The Beginning of My Spiritual and Physical Awakening

I looked out of the window at the bright lights of Las Vegas from my hotel room on the strip. I was there on company business, and was in a dreamy, happy state of mind, wondering what my husband was doing at home in Indiana, in the city known by its local residents as the City of Churches. The lights on the Vegas strip were so radiant and so numerous that I could have been gazing out into the middle of the day, except it was the dark desert night. The late-night brilliance of the Las Vegas 'sun' only added to the surreal events of my day.

The year was 1988, four years after I had read my first book on spiritual awakening, and today was the first day I experienced what I could only identify as my first spiritual / physical awakening. It was happening here, of all places, in Sin City. At the same time, unbeknownst to me, my husband of nine years was experiencing his first sexual affair as he climbed into our bed with his secretary. In the City of Churches, of all places. So it happened that the first day of my awakening was the first day of the beginning of the end of my marriage. And I did not know that either simultaneous event was occurring.

My life had been going great. I was married and working for a major communications company in Indiana, determining how the company would assimilate microcomputers into its organization. My being married was the realization of my mother's dream, while my career was my attempt at realizing my own dream. It was a high profile job. I was in my late 20s, making good money, and I loved the work. But I felt unfulfilled and empty. Something important in my life was missing. I was longing for an experience that would rescue me from the boredom that had been creeping into my life since leaving college and marrying.

During my college years, I had felt so alive—laughing with friends, studying, working, meeting interesting people, dating. In college, I had developed a good sense of self. I was a part of a community with my friends, and saw myself as intelligent, an attribute that I had never before recognized. However, after college and after taking on what I saw as adult responsibilities— including a marriage, a career, and a home life—I was feeling restricted. This restriction unbeknownst to me was self-imposed from belief systems that were not of my own but those I had adopted from family and my culture in order to feel a part of and accepted by those people and structures around me.

Now, I had begun to sense that money, material objects, a career, or a good relationship could not fulfill me. This idea became the basis of my soul searching and my eventual return to the study of psychology, a subject I had loved since the age of 16. Even though I had enrolled in a graduate program, my interest seemed to lie in something more esoteric. Until this time, my attention had been on my marriage and my husband. I did just enough at my job to be considered a good employee, though did not really perform at my potential, because my real focus was on the marriage and the man to whom I was married—until the longing began. That longing led to my betrayal of the marriage and my husband, as I turned my attention toward and gave energy to this important interest of awakening. My husband felt this loss, for his need to have my undivided support and attention was great . . . but we will get to that story later.

In my hometown of 10 years, steepled churches exist on all

four corners of many of the intersections in the downtown area. Only fast-food restaurants outnumber the churches. Residents called my town the City of Churches, but nationally it was known for something entirely different: A national survey had reported its population had the lowest level of intelligence compared to the populations of 50 similar-size cities in all 50 states.

USA Today had interviewed residents about the characterization of this city as a place of low intellect and fast-food feasters. One college student was quoted as saying, 'I knew we were the fattest city, but I did not know we were the dumbest.' Marketers used the City of Churches as a test Market for new fast-food products. Everyone in town, it seemed, was family orientated. Even the university catered to the adult family, structuring their classes to support the working individual and not the recent high school graduate.

Perhaps it was because of this setting that four years earlier, when I had heard about a 'unique' bookstore, I was intrigued and decided to pay it a visit. I had been brought up as fundamentalist Baptist, but I had always been drawn to the unusual, the unique, the controversial, and anything that flew in the face of religious convention.

I drove into town to see if anything on the shelves of this unusual bookstore would quiet my unrest and stimulate my interest. Then, I found this bookstore in its subterranean location. I walked down several stairs to the front door, which was painted blood, 'Scorsese' red. Whether the bookstore's locale contributed to its ominous presence, or whether it was just my own intuition that I was about to enter a stage in my life that would present me with seemingly insurmountable challenges, I felt a combination of anxiety and excitement as I walked down those steps and through that red door.

An Encounter in the Bookstore

A tinkling bell announced my arrival. The store was devoid of people, except for one small clerk who scurried in from an adjoining room. He was shorter than my 5'2", and wore a wrinkled white shirt and too-baggy pants that clung precariously to his hips, beneath a belly that threatened to spill over what I imagined to be a belt creased with buckle marks that chronicled the steady growth of his girth. He wore a loosely knotted tie, as if attempting to appear normal, but the intended effect was offset by the crystal that dangled from the knot. He had an annoying habit of clearing his throat and sniffing every few minutes, keeping time with a severe tic that distorted his face into a grimace. All of these mannerisms belied the peaceful persona he was trying to project.

This bookstore was tiny in comparison to the mega-conglomerate, combination latté and music-selling bookstores that were springing up all over the community. It had only two rooms that were lined from floor to ceiling with books. On the floor was heavy, plush, grass-green carpeting so pristine that it seemed as though few people had walked on it.

My first thought was, how do they stay in business? But those thoughts slipped away when I stared in amazement at the odd and bizarre titles of the books, none of which I had seen on any *New York Times* bestseller list, or in other local bookstores, or even in the City of Churches libraries. There was even a book that the local library had banned due to its un-Christian claim that Jesus had not been crucified, but instead had lived a long life married to Mary Magdalene. There were books on mythology, paranormal psychology, crystal healing, tarot, meditation, Buddhism, Hinduism, Judaism, and all the 'ism' religions, as well as Christianity and Zen.

I found the psychology / parapsychology section, and hungrily devoured the jacket covers of many books. Finally, I settled on a general book on extrasensory perception, believing that maybe if I could increase my sensitivity to the world, my boredom with life would slip away. But by the time I reached the register, I realized I was not satisfied with my selection, so I handed the clerk the ESP book and followed a strong compulsion to walk to the back of the store. There, I reached for a book that I had not seen before.

Dr. Brugh Joy, a physician, healer, and philosopher who had rebelled against traditional medicine, giving up his successful career as a medical doctor to study consciousness, was the author of *Joy's Way*. I did not foresee at all that I, too, would discover a similar path, giving up a rewarding occupation and striking out to live a completely different life, one at which my mother would be aghast.

If I had known this huge change was about to occur—being the person I was at that time, that is, someone afraid of risking marriage, money, and career—I would have replaced the book and quickly walked out, thinking I had found yet another store with nothing to offer. Instead, I did not even read the cover of *Joy's Way* or peruse the pages. Even the picture on the cover of hands surrounded by an aura of light slightly turned me off. I just took it off the shelf and said to myself, 'This is the book,' and walked to the register.

Had I known that this purchase would open me up to a multi-dimensional, unfamiliar world, one that existed on an inner plane that was as every bit as real as the physical world, if I had been armed with the knowledge that I was to turn my current world topsy-turvy in a few short years, I would have stopped in my tracks. I would not have listened to the urging, and would have returned instead to the place of unconscious living where I had pretty much spent my entire life. I would have gone on accepting the essence of life as cause and effect, believing that I think and then I proceed to make it happen.

Fortunately, I was not privy to any of this information. I now believe that there is a certain orchestration that occurs to keep particular facts beyond our awareness, so that we are able to continue down a specific road to an undisclosed destination. For if we were aware of these things, we would go screaming, with arms flailing, back into the familiar darkness and the life from which we came, never again to venture forth. But somehow I encountered an aspect of myself that wanted what this book contained.

Within a few short years, I would leave behind all the structures of security that I had built for myself through my career and marriage. Like the innocent fool who steps to the edge of a precipice and then takes the necessary leap into an illusionary void that has no footing, I did not realize that I had begun a journey of psychological transformation and was being drawn into the initiation stages of this transformation. I became like Alice in Wonderland who fell down the rabbit hole. The world ceased to operate as it had in the past. I could no longer make things happen in my world by sheer motivation. Things ceased to be what they seemed, and I knew they would never again be as they had once appeared. The world as I knew it was over the second I reached for that book . . . and I did not have a clue.

Joy's Way would open me up to seeing the world differently, a world of energy, and to seeing the psyche as made up of multiple selves or multiple dimensions. It would give me the resource of heart-centered awareness. Within a short time after reading Brugh's story, I was practicing the heart-centered awareness that he describes in his book and lives in his own life. Heart-centering became one tool that allowed me to maneuver and traverse my way through the awakening process and avoid many of the pitfalls one encounters when choosing to awaken.

The Matrix: Desire and Commitment to See Beyond Illusion

One of the themes in the movie 'The Matrix' relates to this first stage of awakening in many people's lives, when they begin the process of perceiving and living life completely differently than they had before (Wachowski, 1999). Early in the movie, we see a few qualities that a person requires in order to begin and to stay the course of an awakening process. These characteristics are desire, commitment, and the ability to see truth. The movie's main character, Mr. Johnson, has lived his life in a robot-like way, following the script of a program that had been developed by an unknown source. Mr. Johnson believes he makes his own choices and creates his existence. This theme suggests that free will does not exist when one lives largely unconsciously. Rather, as the movie demonstrates, it is our unconscious dynamics that co-create with existence. We are just following a set of patterns, lived over and over, that our ego develops in order to take the path of least resistance.

Mr. Johnson becomes driven by his need to know about a notorious man named Morpheus. (Morpheus literally means death or transformation.) Morpheus realizes that by changing one's beliefs about and understanding of the world, one can move beyond the restrictions of the ego-driven, physical realm that the self initially encounters. Morpheus is only able to find and connect to Mr. Johnson through Mr. Johnson's desire to seek a deeper process in life, to know the truth. *It is our desire for transformation and truth that begins to bring about the events that support this change in direction.* In this way, desire is the key to initiating the awakening process. Mr. Johnson's all-consuming desire to meet Morpheus leads him eventually to encounter his hero. Mr. Johnson decides to accept Morpheus' challenge to awaken to the 'real world,' and not continue in the illusion by which he had been living his life.

Living life in the illusion means living life without testing the ego self, which is driven to feel safe, in control, in power, and to obtain the goals that will fulfill its needs, such as basic life requirements of food and security, and social requirements of approval, recognition, social acceptance, and success. Living life in the illusion means living life from a heavily defended ego, which is needed to protect the self from deep fear and anxiety, especially from the undifferentiated chaotic energy of the unrealized dimension of existence. The desire to move beyond illusion usually is driven by an existential need, such as a person's urge to understand death, life, transformation, God, or even just to know one's inner self in order to discover peace.

An element within 'The Matrix' shows the relationship between Mr. Johnson, representing the unconscious man, and Morpheus, who symbolizes transformation into a larger perspective and a higher creative aspect of living. In Mr. Johnson's case, he desires something more in his life. Then, through his introduction to Morpheus, life begins to reflect back to him that something more can be had. Another subtle, key element in the movie takes place when Morpheus offers Mr. Johnson the choice to awaken, telling him that he is only offering the truth, nothing more. He does not say, 'It will be easy,' or 'You will have all you desire.' Instead, Morpheus states that the only certainty of awakening is just the truth. As discussed in Chapters 1 and 2, this is all that can really be promised. No obtaining of material riches or ego desires. The various awakening experiences of my friends demonstrate this. The one support a guide or teacher can offer is the tools to prepare a person for his / her awakening experience, which can thereby increase the quality of that experience. Moving beyond illusion and into truth usually comes on the heels of many hours spent in reflection, a practice that increases our desire for transformation and our knowledge of truth. The type of individual who lives life at this depth has at his / her core personality the characteristics of strength, will, compassion, enjoyment, and intuition. Those qualities will be called upon and serve the individual well when he / she does transformation work.

Carl Jung, in his final work, *Mysterium Coniunctionis* (vol. 14 of his *Collected Works*), saw desire as the fire of libido, the energy that is created when the ego separates the self from an object. 'Object' means anything, such as a person, situation, symbol, or image that one sees as existing outside, separate from his / her self. This energy of separation contains desirousness, which is vital in generating life-force creative energy.

Ego-centered desirousness, as contrasted with Self-centered desirousness (with a capital S, to differentiate it from the small, ego self), has often at its basis unconscious, infantile demands for what it wants and when it wants it—usually now. These demands have at their base, fear. When a person indulges in this type of desire, whether it is based in the appearance of good (false love that arises out of fear) or evil (fear), it serves to inflate the ego. It also serves to separate us from the fear, whether that fear is expressed in the appearance of good or evil. Then, when a person obtains the object, he / she feels either unfulfilled, or else the fulfillment is fleeting. Jung saw this striving to achieve the desired object as an individual's 'thirsting for the eternal', while not knowing how to obtain the eternal. The Self-centered desire is a true or a philosophical desire, one that can motivate and provide access to the transformational process that Jung refers to as the *coniunctio*, or the transcending of ego-centered desirousness. Self-centered desire does not have as its motivation a fear of the finality of death but an interest in expressing the deepest divine mystery of the individual in temporality.

Jung's notion of desirousness is illustrated in 'The Matrix'. Mr. Johnson's wish to understand this deeper life process opens for him the portal of the *coniunctio* process of transformation, thus resulting in his meeting with Morpheus (or 'death and transformation'). Mr. Johnson is given the choice of swallowing a red pill or a blue pill. The latter would allow him to fall asleep and to live his life from the same perception that he has always had, a perception that was ego driven, ego defended, and defined. He would repeat the same predictable patterns, be motivated by ego desires, and be influenced by his society and culture.

The red pill would awaken him to a way of perceiving life completely differently, and would entail a journey of great suffering in its endeavor to free the ego from its drives, needs, attachments, and desires. Either decision Mr. Johnson makes would be fine. It is just a matter of how he wants to live. 'The Matrix' demonstrates the darkness and desolation of this awakened landscape for the character Mr. Johnson, who then becomes known as Neo (meaning re-birth) when he swallows the red pill. This also flies in the face of new age spiritual awakening notions of all light, love and beauty.

Many of my friends upon hearing I was writing a book on consciousness, indicated to me to speak the truth regarding what occurs during and after an awakening experience. They told me not to write of the experience as all inspirational and light and all from a one-sided point of view. Awakening initially can be exciting, a rebirth and a perceiving of life differently. Often times you feel energized as if you had been running on an 8 volt battery and now you have plugged into a nuclear power plant. This increase of energy does have its downside, as all things do, and that is when this powerful energy comes up against all the ego's fears and defenses. This is the time when life becomes not easy and reflects back to us our unconscious material.

In a secondary story line in The Matrix, another character, Cypher, also chooses the red pill, discovers that the awakened life is initially challenging and difficult, and bargains with the source of the illusory world to fall asleep again.

Cypher: 'I know what you're thinking, 'cause right now I'm thinking the same thing. Actually, I've been thinking it ever since I got here: Why oh why didn't I take the blue pill? (speaking to Neo, after Neo awakens).

Then in a conversation with the agents of the matrix, who maintain the illusionary world, while having dinner in the matrix,

Cypher: 'You know, I know that this steak doesn't exist. I know when I put it in my mouth, the Matrix is telling my brain that it is juicy and delicious. After nine years, do you know what I've realized? Ignorance is bliss.'

Agent Smith: 'Then we have a deal?'

Cypher: 'I don't want to remember nothing. Nothing! You understand? And I want to be rich. Someone important. Like an actor. You can do that, right?'

Agent Smith: 'Whatever you want, Mr. Reagan.'

As this plot element illustrates, commitment is necessary in order to stay the course, as one begins to challenge the defense structures of the ego and discover liberation from beliefs and patterns that no longer serve one well. Unlike the character Cypher, I have found the journey well worth the effort as it has given me a fulfillment that living unconsciously could not have provided.

Choosing between the Red and the Blue Pill

Like the individual who regrets his decision to awaken, some may interpret Mr. Johnson's decision to proceed with awakening as ill fated, a determination that will bring about strife, crisis, and ultimately unhappiness. Such people see the other choice, to remain unconscious, as the happiest and easiest of the two options, simply because in living this type of life one is rarely aware of one's suffering. The purpose of a heavily defended ego is to separate one's self from fear and anxiety, but this fear is illusory in nature, as it is not born from an actual threat to one's safety. One only feels some semblance of control when one lives at the surface level of existence, believing in the illusion or distraction of what has been created. For many, this semblance of control is enough.

This creation may take the form of pursuing a career, supporting a family, taking part in human dramas, keeping so busy that no quiet time exists for reflection on one's experience.

Like my tsunami experience, anything can be used as a distraction for the ego. Many people manipulate their surroundings as a way of achieving a sense of happiness, which places the control of their well-being into the manipulated object. They have placed their power in an object / person that exist outside of self and that they may have little control over. These individuals have thoughts of, 'I will be happy if I have the right job or the right partner.' They move from relationship to relationship, or from job to job looking for that elusive happiness. Yet they are actually manipulating the object (job or relationship), while believing that their contentment lies within that object. As long as the manipulated object continues to be manipulated, then all is well in the world for such people.

The un-awakened are distracted by the dramas they create in their lives and with others. These crises serve to keep their fears at bay or are the result of their fears creating through them. Even the act of attaining goals in life, such as material possessions, becomes a means not to feel the innate fear of existence or nonexistence and the suffering that accompanies such fear. This was the message I received in my 'tsunami experience'.

Then there is the seduction of choosing to swallow the red pill. This temptation may consist of a spiritual advisor or teacher telling a person that by following and exploring his / her bliss, life will reflect that blissful existence, and that he / she will obtain everything he / she desires in the way of a partnership, career, spiritual and material or psychological gain. All that is needed is meditation and to say affirmations. Of course, this seduction will set a person up for a major betrayal when he / she discovers that living an awakened life is far from the ego's desires and wishes. Seduction serves to entice the insecure ego into making that initial leap.

A person's choosing to awaken does not take into account the vastness of the unconscious dynamics on both the personal and collective levels, or the enormity of the task of consciously carrying the suffering that appears along with these dynamics. But the unconscious has a way of singing the sirens' song, seducing the conscious mind into making a commitment to explore the darkness of one's soul. Seduction becomes necessary because few individuals have the courage to willingly take on the suffering that is required to live consciously. It is the waving of the carrot or the beating of the stick that initially drives one along the path of awakening.

Inanna: Strength, Courage, Desire, and Commitment to Continue Forth

Myths throughout world literature tell of man's entering into states that are more conscious and achieving wisdom typically through crisis. The only known myth in which the main character decides to go knowingly into the underworld dynamics of the soul is that of Inanna, Queen of Sumaria. Inanna, who lived in approximately 2000 B.C., is queen both of the Light and the Dark. Her story is the first known written text discovered on stone tablets. It is also the first tale that describes the tasks or stages that an individual has to move through or master in order to obtain knowledge and wisdom: Integrative Consciousness. This story emphasizes the character's qualities of desire and commitment that were discussed earlier, and also includes new qualities of strength and courage. The myth of Inanna suggests that what is needed to live an awakened life is the stripping away all of the ego's defenses, such as material possessions, false loves, false identities to power, all addictions, the refusal to see below the surface, and finally, the attachment to identity.

In the story, Inanna (an actual Sumarian queen) rules Sumaria with courage and strength. She is an intelligent monarch who also owns the riches and receives the praise that her position as queen affords her. In her experience as queen, Inanna has built the ego strength and courage needed to move forward to the next stage of development. She begins to desire something that her status, riches, and power cannot provide.

Such a yearning usually motivates us to begin our search. Inanna asks her trusted servant to stand witness at the door of the underworld, just in case she needs help. This action tells us the importance of developing a witness aspect of our psyche that will assist with the challenges we may encounter as we enter into the underworld of our consciousness. Heart-centered awareness provides this 'witnessing' aspect of our journey.

Dressed in all her finery and wearing her crown, Inanna knocks on the door to the underworld, demanding to be admitted, as only a queen could demand. Very few people who are living a satisfied life, having their needs met, and are not in a crisis willingly enter into such an underworld process. Inanna's unrest and longing for inner fulfillment become her motivating factors. Her regalia symbolizes that before one makes the journey into the unconscious, the ego must be seated in strength, desire, and commitment. Once granted entry, Inanna begins her descent into the underworld where she journeys to save her dark sister, Ereskigal. Ereskigal represents all the aspects Inanna has not accepted or is not in touch with inside herself.

In the course of her journey, Inanna has to release all of her attachments to material riches, let go of the characteristics that feed the ego, relinquish all desires that are of the ego, challenge the fears the ego defends against, and finally release the last attachment, her identity and self-image as a woman and even as the queen. The significance of this final connection is that we must work through the fear of not having an identity. In our modern day, this typically means letting go of what it means to be someone—a teacher, lawyer, student, wife, husband, father, or mother. By giving up such roles, we come into touch with our insignificance.

In the myth, Inanna surrenders to all that is asked of her. Once she is vulnerable, stripped of everything, then her dark sister,

Ereskigal, kills her and leaves her on her deathbed for three days. This episode represents the tasks that every ego must face in releasing defenses and attachments, each one requiring the surrender to and death by the dark sister, that is, the complete acceptance of the darkness within us. This moment also demonstrates the importance of the role vulnerability plays in the transformation. Many people misperceive vulnerability as being an aspect of weakness, when in actuality it is the ability to be open to *what is*, knowing that one is in partnership with the creative enfoldment of life. Vulnerability is an essential element in the transformation process.

In the myth, the trusted servant becomes worried when Inanna does not return in three days and requests assistance from one of the Gods, Enki, who has always been loyal to Inanna and watched out for her safety. Enki sends a rescue team that brings Inanna back to life after she acknowledges completely her shadow sister. This scene tells us that once that level of ego surrender and sacrifice has been achieved and experienced for an allotted amount of time, then the grace of God is allowed. Inanna then returns to the world above to reign with courage, strength, intuition, and wisdom—all the characteristics of living in the present moment, consciously aware.

Thus, the myth of Inanna describes the process of awakening through the descent mysteries. The descent mystery is the process or journey one takes when beginning to explore one's unconscious material and one's Soul mystery. Typically, this examination involves dark, shadow aspects of our psyche that we have disowned or do not want to recognize. For Inanna, this descent relates to the sacrifice of ego attachments, the acceptance of the dark aspects of the self, the stripping away of false structures, the development of a witness state of consciousness, the ability to be present with the vulnerability of one's fears, the willingness to endure the suffering that occurs, and the surrender to and death of the dark aspects of the self until the grace of God retrieves us from our deathly embrace. Finally, then, we begin anew, with different laws of living that issue from a mind imbued with wisdom. To undergo this type of process requires a strong commitment to stay the course when the goal of Integrative Consciousness is truly undefined initially. For the person going through this process does not know what Integrative Consciousness looks or feels like, as he / she has never before experienced this state.

I believe that, at first, I was enticed into swallowing the awakening red pill by the seductive power of promises of a fulfilled and happier life, a life of living my bliss, and a life of purpose and control, free of fear and anxiety. I bought into the idea that with positive thoughts and the belief I could obtain anything I was lacking in my life, that life would reflect those riches back to me by manifesting them in the form that I chose. Instead, what I discovered is a life liberated from the constraints of ego and the opening up of many, many more possibilities of joy as well as serenity.

Therefore, I embarked on this spiritual journey from an ego-gratifying, carrot-swinging motivation of obtaining success, fame, and fortune, and at the very least, release from boredom. I did not understand then the tremendous effort, discipline, and commitment one has to have in life to 'free up the ego', release the surface ego's defenses, and find total acceptance of the expression of one's being, no matter how different from the ego's vision is that expression. In the awakened state, the ego learns to defer to life forces and to co-create with life, not to 'lord over' and make things happen to satisfy its baser needs or loftier goals. Luckily, my desire and commitment were much larger than the suffering required to go through this process, and the reward of feeling liberated was well worth the effort.

What I find misleading in 'The Matrix' is that the main character, Mr. Johnson, has a distinct moment in which he 'chooses' to go down that path of awakening. I am not sure that this generally happens to individuals, or at least that the moment is distinct enough to allow one to ponder the question and make a deliberate decision. I personally did not have that conscious moment of choice. I did not say to myself, 'Oh, I think I will awaken.' My awakening just occurred in a series of events and I firmly believe is orchestrated by the Self. But, after that day when I stood in the bookstore with *Joy's Way* in my hand, my subsequent explorations would take on a depth and a meaning that I had never before experienced. That day would make all that would soon follow well worth the effort, pain, and loss that one undergoes in the awakening process.

Back to the Future: The Awakening

Fast-forward four years from that day in the bookstore. There I was that fated day in Las Vegas on a business trip. I had been meditating daily since my first reading of Joy's Way. By this time, I had become sensitive to not only understanding that our bodies and minds consist of energy but also feeling this energy around me. My daily practice was to meditate and work to heighten my sensitivity to the energy that I felt in my body, in others, and in my experiences. I sought to live life consciously with serenity and compassion. This outlook motivated me to listen to my reactivity in situations, and this practice became my compass. When I reacted strongly to someone or something, I understood I had an internal ego conflict and I would pay attention.

In addition to my regular job as a systems analyst, I had started a small practice in which I completed energy balancing on people. Energy work consists of a practitioner using a focusing technique that directs his / her concentrated energy to another person's energy chakra centers, until that person reached a calm state of consciousness and the centers were balanced in relation to each other. Using my budding sensitivity to energy and the techniques developed by the Healing Touch Foundation and Brugh Joy, I would scan a person's body for energy imbalances, and then, by directing energy through my body, I would bring his / her body into an energetic balance. This practice increased my awareness of my own energy flow within my body.

I do not know whether 'Sin City' was a necessary or contributory aspect to my physical awakening, but what I experienced at that time on a physical level was astounding. Because taxicabs were in great demand by convention goers in the Vegas area that week, I decided to power walk to the convention center every morning. As I walked, I practiced a heart-centered walking meditation. I settled my awareness, or my 'mind's eye' in the center of my chest, holding the focus to the right of my physical heart, and then breathed in and out through this chakra center. Shortly into this practice, I began to feel my whole body vibrate, as if I had stuck my finger into an electric socket, but without the uncomfortable shock. Every cell vibrated in me, and my thought processes became quiet—no wandering mind, no fear. This quiet mind also provided me with feedback that I was not experiencing an anxiety attack. My awareness rode on wave after wave of movement within my body, even as I took in the presenters' lectures, one after another, on the up-and-coming technologies in the computer world.

I entered one room to attend a lecture on parallel processing techniques used in a mini computer system, and as I sat down and crossed my legs I exploded into an orgasm. You might imagine my surprise at this new development and my efforts to hide from the attendees sitting around me the feelings as waves and waves of pleasure coursed through my body.

After this orgasmic experience, I became aware both of the vibration flowing through my body as it had all morning and afternoon and of what was occurring in my external world. I could hear my own voice telling me, 'Stay heart-centered,' and I allowed this energy to move, as it needed to move. This aspect within myself that was the source of this deep knowing was a new and profound experience for me, but it was still and sane in its proclamation.

I knew that something strange and wonderfully miraculous was happening. What I did not realize was that this mind calmness and stillness in the midst of the vibration in my body was a precursor to my descent into the underworld, a major challenge to my marriage, and that soon my ego's unresolved attachments, fears, and beliefs would surface. Initially, though, even with the intense movement of energy inside my body, my mind was strangely quiet. With a still mind, I understood that the vibration I was feeling was not anxiety. Anxiety is borne out of a disquiet fearful ego. Through it all I felt connected to the source of my inner voice, which sounded as if it had knowledge of this happening. I just allowed myself to be an observer, witnessing the energy's flow.

I can appreciate someone who might want to retreat from the world in order to keep the energy flowing, not wanting it to go away. Engaging in daily activities and interacting with others does affect the energy's movement. I was forming an attachment to it that would need to be addressed later, but for the moment I just accepted this physical awakening as an interesting occurrence, without any need to control the process. It did not occur to me to withdraw from the world. My goal always is to integrate my experience by being a part of the world, not escaping into isolation. My motivation is to expand the ego so that I can be in the world, but not be the victim of my personal experiences or those of others.

When I returned to the hotel, I met up with the men I worked with in my organization. Typically on other trips, after the perfunctory dinner, I went off on my own, usually back to the hotel. This time, my colleagues were following me around the casino and hotel in a straight line, like ducklings after their mother, asking me where I was going, what I was going to do next. It was strange to see these grown businessmen acting this way. They evidently wanted to spend the evening in my presence, which was a new experience for me. I do not know if I was exuding raw sexuality, but whatever it was these men wanted to spend the evening with me, which was a unique experience for me. I was quite satisfied with being alone to experience the energy occurring within my body.

I was extremely sexually attracted to one man, in particular. This was the first time I found myself attracted to another man outside of my nine-year marriage. Ben was small in stature, with a kind nature, and he looked like a choirboy, a corporate-America, suited and tie-d version of James Dean. His naughty choirboy persona intrigued me. We had never met in person before, but had had many phone conversations regarding the coordination of our work within the corporation. This was the first time we had met face-to-face, and his interest in me took on a new dimension of strong sexual attraction. Much to my chagrin, I entertained visions of us having a fling in Vegas, and then returning home to our respective spouses, allowing what had happened in Vegas to remain in Vegas.

However, I could not allow this involvement to transpire. As I contemplated it, I knew that the heightened sexuality that was occurring within me had more to do with some type of spiritual or consciousness growth, and was not to be used or directed in a sexual conquest, especially when it meant dealing with the extreme guilt and feelings of distrust over betraying myself, my husband, and our marriage, or diverting my attention away from being present to this energy flow. I had always seen myself as a woman of integrity and loyalty, and I did not want to challenge this image of myself. I might add, however, later in my life and outside the context of this book, my attachment to this image has become tested, as all our self-images do when we reach these later stages of ego development.

I wondered if these intense vibrations and my sexual interpretation were being influenced by the Las Vegas environment. Or had some unconscious, all-seeing, all-knowing aspect within me orchestrated this business trip to Vegas so as to have the Vegas environment / energetic support as its developmental basis? Vegas is a city of strong sexual and base energies that are reflected in the sex, gambling, magic, and escapism in all of their many forms. The city was built exactly for those purposes. It is an oasis for men to break free and find a sense of freedom from life's responsibilities through the enjoyment of women, wine, and the thrill of gambling. Vegas caters to addictions, and here I was, a person not addicted to drugs, alcohol, gambling, or sex.

However, was there a strong addiction that I was not aware of, so that Vegas was a natural place to start this journey to explore whatever addiction ailed me? By then, I had enough understanding of Jung and his philosophy and what it means to be consciously aware. Following this philosophy I understood that events that played out after this Vegas experience would show me the arena in which I would explore my strongest attachment or addiction if one existed. The city was beckoning me to enter her portals and respond to her siren song. Would I have the ability to resist, or better yet, the ability to go forward, allowing the seduction to occur but with my eyes wide open, and to benefit from the experience? Or would my eyes close, lulled to sleep in the seducer's embrace, only to be dashed against the rocks with the subtleness of a slow, gentle tide approaching the shore that obscures the riptides under the surface?

My Marriage as the Stage for My Underworld Drama Play

That evening after returning to the hotel room, I called Steve, my husband, to touch base as I typically would do while on business trips. Steve was quick at humor, tall, and athletic. Our marriage was wonderfully supportive, loving, sexual, easy, and fun. Up until this moment, it had not been challenged by any situation. When I was 21 years old, enjoying my friends and college life, Steve and I had met at a club during the height of the disco era.

Steve had asked me to dance, so out onto the floor we went. I was waiting for Steve to begin, to lead in the dance. Here I was standing still, amid all the swirling and gyrating dancers beneath the mirrored rotating disco ball that was throwing out rays of reflected light into the darkened crowd, when he said, 'You need to show me how to dance.'

We stood in awkward silence, motionless. I did not know how to lead. I had always followed, as is the norm for female dancing partners. Steve had assumed from watching me earlier dancing with a wonderful, experienced dancer that I knew how to dance. So I told him I did not know how, but willing to begin dancing to avoid further embarrassment. My leading the dance was a sign of the structure our relationship would take and a reflection of a masculine polarization that I would explore for many years. For me, this polarization would express in various forms of the strong protector / weak defenseless, or independent / dependent or compentency / incompentency. The degree of conflict reflected the degree of polarization. The polarization and conflict of my internal masculine, both the positive and negative aspected qualities were mirrored in outer males in my life.

Within two months of meeting, Steve and I were engaged, and were married one year later. We both had successful careers, he as an engineer and I as a computer-systems analyst. We made good money that allowed us to travel, invest, and buy anything we wanted.

When I called Steve from Vegas and he answered the phone, I immediately noticed that his voice sounded strained, different.

'How are things going?' I asked.

'Okay.'

'Is there something wrong?' I wondered if he was particularly upset with the fact that I was in Las Vegas, and that I had traveled there with six of my male coworkers. Was he feeling a little threatened about that?

'No. Things are okay.'

His answers were too curt.

'Okay. . . . I wanted to give you a call and wish you a good night.'

'Okay.' I waited for the usual 'I love you,' but there was only an uncomfortable silence on the other end of the line, a pause. We both knew what was expected, but he was failing to deliver. So I took the lead.

'I love you, Steve. I will see you in a couple of days. I will call you tomorrow.'

Again, a long drawn-out silence, he responded, 'I love you, too. Goodbye.'

The conversation left me feeling anxious. We had never had a stilted moment between us. This was new. Initially, I wrote it off as the circumstances of my business trip, or maybe some part of his consciousness was picking up on my increased sexuality. Maybe this new aspect of my being had caused him to feel anxious without his understanding why. As I would soon realize, I always felt responsible for any difficulty in our relationship. By accepting responsibility, I felt I had the power to make changes, to make things right. It gave me a sense of control.

I would never have guessed that during our conversation Steve was in our bed with his office secretary—an affair, absolutely my worst nightmare. My life had been pleasant until the husband I never suspected would betray me told me something that I had never expected to hear. Steve said he was no longer in love with me. He denied that he was involved with another woman. For the next year and a half, I lived in the depths of the underworld dynamics—anguish, despair, fear, anxiety, and pain—all of which became the greatest teaching tools I would ever find.

Therefore, in retrospect, I did respond to the call of the siren. And as fate would have it, I did open my eyes . . . wide.

The Importance of Relationship to Awakening

In the destruction of my marriage, I discovered the importance of interpersonal relationships to the development of consciousness. Relations between other people and myself became the guidepost in my transition from an immature person in my way of connecting to the world, to a mature person with a perspective that allows a level of presence, serenity, awareness, and emotional depth. An immature relationship is filled with manipulations—of others, of a situation, as well as of the self—and is controlled by both subtle and strong emotions that stem from states of consciousness of which we are unaware. Our surface ego is living at a shallow level. These ego-driven aspects do not fully understand intimacy, since intimacy of the depths within us is almost nonexistent to the ego-driven perspective. When we are unconscious, we are not intimate with or even aware of these aspects that reside so deep within us, the aspects that are not ego-gratifying. We do not want to be aware of them as they would give us a negative slant of how we perceive ourselves or place us in the position of empowerment that the risks become too great. In fact, we have disowned many of these aspects. We do not 'really know or love' ourselves, so how can we really know or love another? When living at the surface, then, we are not conscious of our fears and the true motivations behind our actions.

Intimacy with the self does not exist when our awareness is entirely surface ego-centered, so neither can intimacy with another person exist. These immature, ego-driven aspects, or states of consciousness, which are based in fear, have strong *reactions* to others and situations. Therefore, free choice does not exist, since our response is determined by the other and at unconscious levels. When we simply react, we do not have free will, and the quality of our experiences is in direct relationship to the people and the circumstances around us.

Even though I had much understanding of the workings of the mind through intellectual pursuits and philosophies that taught me to see the world differently, these teachings did not address my reactive emotional attachments and limited belief systems. My marital conflicts became the best classroom or seminar that I had ever attended.

I was learning how to read the unconscious through seeing it reflected in all my relationships, whether it was my personal relationships to other people or an abstract relationship such as my work or objects. I was learning how those connections established themselves into patterns that would repeat over and over. I was not only surprised but also fascinated by my continually repeating the patterns that caused more suffering for others and myself. I was learning how my reactivity in those relationships determined my consciousness development, and could provide me with the road map to a more developed state of consciousness.

The key, as I understood it, was that coming into consciousness was about the quality of those interpersonal attachments, about my moment-to-moment intellectual and emotional awareness of them, as well as my ability to interact, not react, in relational situations. *Consciousness seemed to emerge from this awareness and acceptance of my interpersonal relationships to objects, situations, and people.* This is not a statement to be taken lightly. The depth of nonjudgmental acceptance of our reactive perceptions of situations, people, and objects determines where we are on this road of becoming, of becoming conscious.

Unfortunately for us, becoming conscious usually is accompanied by a great deal of suffering, enough so that many people abandon the path of awakening to return to a life over which they believe they have control and power, even if that sense is only an illusion. Although suffering exists in any awakening process, by employing practiced techniques and awareness, a person can endure his / her suffering as well as shorten the experience. The result is an increased quality of life that is well worth the effort.

Chapter Five

The Integrative Consciousness Process

Each experience has its own velocity according to which it wants to be lived, if it is to be new, profound, and fruitful. To have wisdom means to discover this velocity in each individual case.

Rainer Marie Rilke, Letters to a Young Poet

In order to proceed to a fuller understanding of Integrative Consciousness, it is important to understand key terms used in this discussion. I offer here a brief overview of these terms, and then in later chapters, a more detailed exploration, discussing the theory, concepts, and research behind Integrative Consciousness, as well as my own experiences in applying Integrative Consciousness techniques.

I have thus far used the terms 'mind' and 'psyche' inter-changeably. I define psyche as a 'subjectively perceived functional entity, comprised of complex conscious and unconscious processes that operate beyond the physical and which govern the total organism and its interaction with the environment' (Siegel, 1999, p. 2). Based on this definition, then, the conscious and unconscious processes that control the individual's responses to the environment allow us to use this interaction as a means to bring into awareness those processes that we typically do not have knowledge of. This interaction becomes the key to understanding our unconsciousness, and can be employed as a great tool for awareness.

This definition brings several questions to mind: What are the processes that exist outside the physical realm and that control the individual? Many people believe that they act of their own free will. Does the idea of a governing force support this belief in free will, even though the two concepts appear to be contra-dictory? Is it only an illusion that we have free will, and are we correct in the presumption that anyone can see, measure, or scientifically observe these governing forces that reside beyond the physical? How do we become aware of the processes that operate outside of our awareness and that have the power to determine our interactions with the environment? Can we truly not be aware of the influences of the subconscious, believing we are acting from conscious free will? Or does our subconscious actually hold sway over us? Let us explore these questions.

Integrative Consciousness

Working in my own personal daily reflective practice, as well as with hundreds of clients over the years, I now understand how deeply unconscious we are in our actions. Brugh Joy (1997) has said that we are 98 percent unconscious. If this is true, then there is a vast world to explore about which we are truly unaware and which exists within us.

Integrative Consciousness, as I have experienced it, is a process that occurs within the aspect of the psyche that is uncon-scious, and that, once achieved, allows an individual to have nonreactive interactions in situations with other people. 'Nonreactive' interactions means that there is no internal conflict or defensive struggle of the ego, and that actions taken from this state come from a conscious place of clarity and emotions, a place of stillness and co-creating with life, the result of Integrative Consciousness.

Integrative Consciousness proposes a different state of perceiving the world, not the same perception that we generally have of recognized thoughts, running commentary, images, beliefs, and views. Integrative Consciousness—or other terms used to describe this state, such as Presence (Tolle, 1999, p. 14) or whole consciousness (Edinger, 1994, p. 19)—is the process of obtaining a state of awareness that, if it occurs at all, emerges in adulthood. It involves an awareness of that which is beyond the physicality of existence and the actions of others, does not relate to situations from past object relations, and involves an acceptance of what is. As we will see, awareness and acceptance are two vital components of Integrative Consciousness. Rarely do individuals explore or obtain awareness and acceptance that lead to integration, a third component, and resonance, a fourth element of Integrative Consciousness.

Awareness involves learning to discern the responses of the body, mind, and emotions as you interact with life in the moment, as described in the definition above. A way to discover your body / mind reactions is to listen to how you relate to other people and situations, especially in your intimate relationships. You can learn a great deal about your unconscious material by developing the ability to perceive the quality of your relationship interactions.

The second component, *acceptance*, is key to the process of breaking through the defensive structures of the ego that prevent Integrative Consciousness. Integrative Consciousness does not occur if the ego is in defense. The ego will employ defensive structures if its existence is threatened. Acceptance involves surrendering to what is happening in the moment, without attachments to what should be happening or to a future outcome. The heart-centered state of consciousness is the resource that assists with acceptance. Obtaining the first and second components results in the third element of the process, *Integrative Consciousness*.

A person achieves Integrative Consciousness when the larger state of consciousness absorbs the defenseless and vulnerable ego structure. When this integration occurs, our thoughts diminish and anxiety quiets, as ruminating thoughts and anxiety are the result of a defended ego. We become less reactive to people and situations, which in turn leads to a higher quality of personal experiences. Our thought processes become progressively more focused and clear. We have stillness.

Resonance, the fourth component of the Integrative Consciousness process, is the product of an evolved ego that has integrated many aspects that were fear based in the past. Resonance is the ability, along with courage, compassion and strength, to be present with another's suffering, without the ego moving into a defensive structure. After an individual reaches Integrative Consciousness with a structure, then the next challenge becomes to carry that suffering for another person as he/she struggles with the same structure. When one person carries another's suffering, this process alone allows the other person to find acceptance for their situation, and eventually results in the transformation of the structure for both parties. For example, if you transform greed within yourself, then you are able to accept greed in another person. This acceptance begins to allow the other person struggling with greed to find self-acceptance and eventually transform his or her own greed. I regard resonance as a step one takes toward providing service to others.

I will discuss and explore in more detail the components of awareness, acceptance, and resonance in later chapters.

Duality States of Consciousness

Understanding the processes of Integrative Consciousness is easier when one comprehends the developing ego's way of perceiving the world, which issues from a state of duality.

Carl Jung viewed the ordinary state of consciousness, a state ruled by the ego, as that of duality, the polarization of opposites (1973, 14: para. 206). He illustrates the function of opposites in his *Mysterium Coniunctionis*:

The factors, which come together in the coniunctio, are conceived as opposites, either confronting one another in enmity or attracting one another in love. To begin with, they form a dualism; for instance—the opposites are moist / dry, cold / warm, upper / lower, spirit-soul / body, heaven / earth, fire / water, bright / dark, active / passive, volatile / solid, precious / cheap, good / evil, open / occult, east / west, living / dead, masculine / feminine, sol / Luna (p. 10).

Let us attempt to understand Jung's Mysterium material, as it can be difficult. We will discuss the essential information that can provide the foundational work for your own transformational process.

Typically, the young or immature person views the world in opposites—cold / hot, mean / kind, control / no control, hate / love, sad / happy. These opposites constitute the basic anatomy of the ego. The polarization of opposites generates psychic energy. Edinger (1994) uses the analogy of comparing this state to electricity moving between the positive and negative poles of an electrical circuit. As in the electrical circuit, when we separate an object into negative and positive poles, then we have created a space in our consciousness that contains energy. This energy is the libido of life. Our attraction to or avoidance of an object that our ego has separated out generates psychic energy, and is the motivation underlying most of our actions (Edinger, 1994, pp. 11-12). This separation becomes the impetus, or the fuel, for how we create in the world. Most people operate from a duality perspective of the world. This dualistic viewpoint is referred to as consensus reality.

Jung's Coniunctio Process
Jung (1973) speaks of coniunctio as the process of those opposites coming together (14: para. 778). Coniunctio means wholeness, so we are talking about achieving wholeness of consciousness, in other words, Integrative Consciousness. Therefore, the linking up of opposites is an essential step toward Integrative Consciousness. This undertaking is the major developmental task of the mature ego.

Jung (1973) sees ego separation as a process of the young ego, a step that is required in order to develop and strengthen the ego to increase self-esteem, and to provide the foundation for a later process of the union of opposites (14: para. 203). This union, the bringing together of the separated parts, occurs in post-ego development, and is a process that few people undertake. When individuals have identified with more positive than negative qualities, then they have created a strong ego, an essential aspect needed to successfully undergo the later developmental stages of ego.

An initial and important stage of awareness is the realization that we have identified with a pole or a construct, and disowned or distanced ourselves from its opposite pole. When we are reactive to a pole, we identify with its opposite, which is the pole more acceptable to our ego. Such identification is a defense mechanism to protect us from the threat associated with the other pole. Thus, once you realize you are reactive to a situation, person, or object, then you know that you are involved in an ego separation / defensive process. When you discern that you have identified with one pole and separated from the other, you know that you harbor some fear in association with the other, and that you have idealized the identified pole.

For example, if you hate selfishness in people and hold in esteem its opposite, generosity, then you have polarized the self in this dynamic. Your ego has identified with generosity (sees it as good) and separated itself from selfishness (sees it as bad). This means that selfishness is a threat to your ego, while generosity strokes your ego with power and confirmation. While this system serves the ego in the initial developmental stages, it becomes an obstacle when the ego moves into later maturation.

However, why would one not want to identify with generosity, one might ask. On an outward behavioral level, it appears to be a good gesture. Yet, our generosity can arise from the need to distance ourselves from our selfishness and therefore our generosity is *fear based*. To uncover what underlies this separation, we might explore what could be the fear of selfishness. For example, perhaps we act generously in order to avoid feeling bad because we are in fact selfish. Or when we go into selfishness, we begin to get in touch with the fear of not having enough in order to survive. However, if you desire wholeness–consciousness–this distancing masks the underlying ego threat, and maintains ego defenses. The distancing from selfishness that comes from being generous keeps your ego defense engaged with the fear of selfishness. You do not see it because you have identified with generosity, and therefore you feel good about yourself. Nevertheless, you are not conscious of your relationship to selfishness and generosity. Ego defenses prevent the Integrative Consciousness process with that structure, in this case the union of selfishness and fear-based generosity.

Oftentimes before the union of the opposites can occur, a person needs to experience both polar aspects many times over. Like the swinging of the pendulum from one pole to the other, we take on the opposites. This pendulum process paves the way for moving on to the next steps in this union of the opposites, which are surrender or complete acceptance, and then finally, integration.

From Duality to Wholeness

Jung (1973) viewed the concept of wholeness of consciousness as the simultaneous experience of opposites and the acceptance of that experience (8: para. 425). The acceptance of what is and the wisdom to understand that experience are evidence that our ego is developing into larger consciousness states and maturing into later developmental stages. This is Integrative Consciousness.

The ego creates dualism when it identifies with one aspect of a structure or a person. When this happens, an individual has separated the structure into two opposite poles. Polarization of opposites usually contains a judgment, that is, an individual separates him- or herself from one pole, allowing the ego to identify with the other, more gratifying pole. Then that individual is in a reactive state to the opposite pole, relating and responding to the world out of an ordinary, consensus or reactive-reality viewpoint. Ninety-eight percent of the world views reality from a duality perspective, while only 2 percent achieve Integrative Consciousness with any perspective.

To summarize, when such a separation occurs with any ego structure, this tells us that at the base of the separated dynamic lies some fear that threatens the ego self. Jung calls consciousness an enduring psychic state created by the union of these opposites. In the case of our example, this would be a union of selfishness and generosity or a dissolving of the fear that these structures arise out of. The integration process can occur instantaneously or take years to complete. If the process occurs over a long time span, this might suggest that we need to experience both aspects of the structure and live those aspects for a while. In other words, returning to the example above, you may need to encounter selfishness for many years, in direct experience of being selfish or in experience of witnessing it in others. Then you may encounter generosity for many more years before you are able to see or get in touch with the fear or a depth of knowledge underlying this structure.

This merging of opposites takes place when we can allow ourselves to be present with the fear of the pole from which we have separated. Looking again at our example of selfishness and generosity, if we can be present with our fear of being selfish, then this may uncover a deeper fear, such as worry over a lack of material security, or even a dread of not having an identity that is defined by material possessions. When the ego is present with fear, it expands enough to contain the dynamic from which we have separated. Therefore, the ego does not need to project the dynamic out onto others. The ego does not need to defend. If we can stay present with the fear of selfishness / generosity without ego defense, then the ego understands there is no threat, and is able therefore to carry the fear without defending. Once this surrender occurs and the ego has dropped its defenses, Integrative Consciousness begins.

The result of the integration is that you are *nonreactive* emotionally and hold no judgment when you see selfishness or generosity displayed in others. You have compassion for people who are involved in the suffering that accompanies the fear underlying selfishness or generosity. You are able to grasp the service this structure has for the person or the collective. When you have compassion with a structure, then ego releases the defense, and the larger state of consciousness absorbs the defense. When one has integrated the dual structure, actions one takes from a place of no defense, meaning no fear or separation from the fear, begin to reflect a generosity that arises from a place of clarity. Therefore, when you have Integrative Consciousness with a structure, there is authenticity behind its expression, your motivations have clarity, and the expression of your consciousness is not used to cover up something else.

Integrative Consciousness in the Corporate World?

A pattern from my own personal history vividly illustrates the Integrative Consciousness process. I began working in the computer industry during the advent of the microcomputer boom in the corporate world in 1980. At this time, I had already spent several years learning microcomputer systems and implementing them into the operations of my company. I was finally familiar and comfortable with this field of technology. Then, my boss assigned me a new project, to phase in minicomputer systems within a seven-state area. This venture would entail my installing the computers that would gather and transfer the information that contained every phone and data call from all customers into the mainframe computer, which would then process and create the company's billing. This undertaking was an integral piece of the company's success because it brought in revenue. The project also had to comply with Federal Communications Commission (FCC) regulations. Due to the project's complexity and my lack of experience working with minicomputer systems, my boss informed me that I would be working overtime, possibly 60-hour weeks.

The term 'chauvinistic male' was widely used in those days, and easily defined my manager. He would say things such as, 'Now that woman over there who was promoted to manager probably slept her way to the top because she sure does not have an ounce of business sense,' while he pointed at an attractive woman who stood in front of the Coke machine, dressed in a nice, professional business suit. I glanced in the woman's direction and wonder if there were any truth to his statement. This wondering alone should have been a clue to my own unconscious beliefs about the abilities of a woman in the business world but the funny thing about the unconscious is that it is…well, unconscious. I understood on an intellectual level that a woman in business was just as effective as a man, but the intellect is not the same as consciousness.

During this time, I was well into developing the concepts and practice behind Integrative Consciousness. I was learning how to be aware throughout the day, and I practiced acceptance of any of the day's conflicts during the evening through heart-centering meditation. My meditation experience now helped me notice an insecurity rise up within myself at the comments my boss made when I took some time to reflect on my day. I was able to identify this anxiety as a child-like aspect that peeked out from behind the Wizard of Oz' curtain that I had created as a facade in order to function in the world, especially the world of business. I did not know that soon the curtain would be pulled back, revealing the frightened, child-like woman operating the controls that kept everyone from seeing just how insecure she was.

Two Defensive Egos Collide

So, I began working on what I will call 'the computer project'. Two men pushing two-wheeled carts hauled box after box of computer manuals into my office. Soon, there was a small path from my door to my chair, and I sat hidden among the stacks of manuals, which actually was fine with me. I really wanted to hide. It was not long before I realized that I had no idea what to do on this project and no clue as to where to start. I turned to my boss for help.

He looked at me and stated with a stern, sarcastic edge to his voice, 'Why, Melissa, you need to develop an implementation plan. Go do your job.'

'Yes, I know. But what are the steps of that plan? I am at a loss here, Brad.'

Then Brad became angry. 'We pay you good money to know what to do. So do it,' he shouted and turned away, staring at papers on his desk. I left his office terrified.

So I opened up a computer manual, placed it on my desk, and sat there with my eyes closed . . . for 8 hours a day, minus the hour for my lunch, of course.

After terror immobilized me for a week, I decided to begin using the tools of consciousness transformation that I had been developing for the last several years, and to get beneath some of the fear I was feeling. I started by sitting with my eyes closed and going into my fear.

First, I re-experienced my reactivity with my manager's anger, and I felt reduced to a child-like stature. I must have been uncomfortable with a man's rage. I had no idea that I was, but as I sat in my reactivity, images of my father's anger that had usually been directed at me kept flashing through my mind. I allowed myself to be present with this feeling without ego defense stepping in to take me out of my experience. Sitting with compassion for little girl, uncomfortable with a man's anger and disapproval.

My ego, being very sly, would enter and say, 'Your boss is just a chauvinist pinhead. Everyone knows what type of man he is. He does not see the value of women.' I would then feel justified in my relations with my boss and almost stop the exercise, thinking I was finished since I no longer experienced my vulnerability. I felt powerful in my justification. Wow, I must have worked through that fear and quickly, too. Then, I had a sudden insight.

How easy it was for me to take myself out of my vulnerability and, once again, to revert to my ego, which was ready to defend against my feeling susceptible. I would stop my ego's commentary by turning my focus back onto my inner experience of fear of a man's anger, his disapproval of me, and my belief that a woman has no value. These were my projections and my unconscious fears that I was transferring to the situation and the relationship with my boss.

Another aspect I perceived in this exchange with Brad was my anxiety that I was incompetent and not intelligent enough to do this work, which was much in alignment with my belief that women had no value. Brad's attitude toward women in business and my feeling, first, uncomfortable, and then my acquiescing to his spoken opinions reflected my sense of my own lack of ability and fear that I lacked the ability. On a conscious level, I regarded myself as an intelligent, independent woman who did not need the approval of anyone to feel good about myself. Yet, what was reflected back to me was the opposite, deeper truth of my belief system. I thought I was not intelligent enough to work competently at anything.

The duality structures of approval / disapproval, competence / incompetence, and intelligence / unintelligence created an internal conflict that played out in my professional life by reducing the extent of my creative pursuits and fostering difficulties in my relationships with male managers. While this separating of these structures within my own ego served me very well through my young adulthood, as I had finished school and landed a very good engineering job, they were preventing me from working effectively with little stress and of course, developing consciously.

Escape to the Monastery Mountain

So I 'sat' with my not being intelligent, and layers of layers of new fears appeared, such as my feeling unloved, and believing I was not able to care or provide for myself. As each fear arose, I stayed present with it. My sly ego would step in and say, 'But, Melissa, you have a college degree. You are intelligent.' I again would reply, 'This may be true, but I need to stay with my vulnerability of not feeling competent,' and then I would return my focus to being present with incompetency. At another stage of development, when one is building self-esteem, the ego defense of grabbing onto my being intelligent would be fine. However, at this point I wanted to move beyond ego-defended, reactive states of consciousness and into conscious living. The concept of who I was, was based in resisting what I feared I would be, the opposite pole. Therefore, the threat or fear of not being intelligent enough and also the sense that I was somehow in danger because of this threat were the illusions I needed to transform.

Each day I would arrive at work at 7:30 a.m., place an open computer manual on the desk, pull up my chair, and close my eyes to do 'consciousness' work. Luckily for me, my boss was not a detailed, hands-on manager, but every now and then his head would rise above the stacks of computer manuals, look down on me, and ask, 'How is it going, Melissa?' and I, looking up, yet unwilling to face his disapproval and anger, would respond, 'It's coming along, Brad.' Then, he would quickly leave before I could say anything more, and walk back to his office.

Of course, outwardly things did not look fine. I was already five weeks into the project and had not done a single outward thing. The deadline for the first computer system to be in place was approaching. Equipment orders needed to written, networks determined and put into place, buildings brought up to code, and people trained to operate the computers; however, I still had no idea where to begin. Yet, something deep inside of me told me that I needed to work through these dynamics and find an internal support system in order to accomplish these tasks and save my job. I did not know how my meditative work was going to assist me in the trouble I found myself in at work, but for the moment, it was all I could do. I had to trust.

My 'Ah-Ha' Moment

And then, it happened. I heard from the computer vendor that they were releasing a larger, more efficient computer system. An idea to redesign the computer network was born, and I spent a few days designing and calculating the cost savings to the company that the new design would offer and putting this information into a proposal to introduce to Brad. I had taken a 28-system network down to seven systems in seven locations, and this restructuring would save the company over eight million dollars during the first two years of implementation.

I took my proposal to Brad, who was in his office. As I was walking in with my arms full of scattered papers, I let him know I had a suggestion to redesign the network. Brad, his face beet-red, looked at me incredulously and screamed, 'Melissa, a team of engineers designed that network. Just do your job!' This scream-like yell alerted others in the office, so that they stopped what they were doing. Heads popped up, and eyes peered over office partitions to see who was the recipient of Brad's wrath. Again, I was reduced to a child-like stature. Humiliated, I turned on my heels and ran back to my office. My 'father' had just chastised me. For the next week, I sat with this feeling, finding deeper compassion for the part of me that fears a man's anger and disapproval.

Once Again, into the Dragon's Den

The deadline was approaching, just two months away, and I knew that I needed to talk with Brad again and attempt to present my proposal. I understood that my fear of disapproval and anger was not a good enough reason for the company to lose millions of dollars. I was also aware that if I did not get the necessary work completed at record-breaking speeds, I would lose my job, Brad would lose his job, and the company would face an unknown amount of fines from the FCC. Yet, for some unknown reason, I was focused on getting this new proposal approved and then I would take a look at implementing the project.

I approached Brad's office in a focused, observer state of awareness (I will discuss this further in the chapter on acceptance). I was slightly anxious, yet I felt strong, as I just allowed myself to observe my anxiety and not identify with that feeling. It was as if the uneasy part of me were walking alongside me, but was not the one in control. I entered Brad's office, and he rose from his chair and began yelling. Then he suddenly paused in mid-yell, and actually looked confused.

I maintained a state of quietness within. I felt no reactivity within myself, no fear of his anger, no fear of his disapproval and no fear of his confusion. The anxious part of me was no longer in my awareness, as I was fully in the moment. All the insecurity I was infused with all those weeks before were, well, gone. There was just stillness, a deep quiet. I had no thoughts, no investment as to the outcome of this impromptu meeting. As I glanced at Brad, he looked like a caricature on one of the large float balloons in the Macy's parade that someone had just let all the air out of. Now the balloon was deflating. I became aware in that moment when I saw the smallness of Brad that Brad was also afraid. I sensed he knew he was about to lose his job if I did not complete this project on time. He did not know how to help me, and I felt compassion toward him as well as toward myself, as I had been there in that fear recently. He then stated, 'Oh, okay. Let's see what you have.' Unbelievable.

After looking at my proposal, he became excited, as if someone had performed CPR and breathed new life into him. He appeared 'inflated' again, and a newfound, confident Brad said, 'We have to get the Vice-President's approval for this redesign, but I think you may have something here.'

Co-Creating Synchronistically

The interesting thing about individuals who work within a corporate environment is their need to be a part of a high profile, successful project that is saving the corporation millions of dollars, especially during the first year of implementation. Once word spread about my redesign, which took about one to two days, I had people telling me exactly what needed to be done and volunteering to help. I completed the implementation of the system on schedule and successfully, with almost no hiccups. As a result of the project's success, managers received their bonuses, and Brad was promoted to another office. For my part, management recognized me at a luncheon. For some reason, this recognition did not matter. I was understanding the power of working with these deeper aspects of the psyche and how to move beyond ego-defended fear. By being present with undefended fear of incompetency and competency and other structures that came into my awareness, I had integrated ego-based, separated structures into some larger state of consciousness. In so doing, I was able to unleash a more creative aspect of my psyche that brought forth the knowledge and recognized opportunities that otherwise would have gone unnoticed to discover innovative solutions to the problem at hand. I now had a reputation as something of an enigma, as I heard whispers of wonder about how I had saved the project at the last minute and redesigned the whole system. All the while, my colleagues were witnessing my earlier struggles and anticipating my failure. Most importantly for me, management gave me permission to take time for meditation whenever I needed, something unheard of for a major corporation in the 1980s: the recognition of the feminine in a masculine world.

A few years later, a coworker told me that she had had lunch with Brad, and that he had bragged that he had made me into the businessperson I had become. And he was right, at least partially.

My relationship with the need for a male's approval and the depths of insecurity I had regarding my abilities initiated a major transformation in me that day in Brad's office, right at the moment of our interaction. When confronted with his anger, my ego did not reach for defense. I had worked with this dynamic in meditation, found acceptance for these aspects of myself, and had made space within the ego to carry Brad's disapproval and fear without my becoming reactive and reduced to a childlike stature. Because I had reached a new state consciously with these fears, I was able to understand Brad's insecurities (also mine) around women and their abilities and maybe even his own insecurity. In that instant, I also held the space for Brad's own suffering, which is the fourth component of Integrative Consciousness: resonance. Resonance is the beginning of a person's ability to assist humanity, as that person becomes able to carry the suffering of others.

I believe that in that moment of my presenting my ideas to Brad in his office, when he did not get the response from me that he would have in the past, then another way began for us to interact with each other. He was unable to manipulate me into getting the power he needed to feel by having me react fearfully. The parts of my ego that had separated into duality structures, in the form of disowned projections and patterns, began the process of integration into the larger state of consciousness. For me, this resulted in a new way of being in my work, and my relationship with Brad improved dramatically. He could no longer obtain power by reducing me to a childlike status, and there was no need for him to. I was not interested in having power over him and had removed myself from his projective eye. I would leave this job and company shortly thereafter, as indicated in my story in Chapter Four, but I left as a success and not as a failure, the later being a possible path I could have traveled.

This last statement is important to understand and reemphasize. There is a seductive power in a widely known theory that if you change your belief system of what you see as possible, then you will obtain what you want out of life. This theory asserts that life reflects back to you what you believe in. This is true, but not in the way most people understand this concept. For example, many of us think that if we see ourselves as worthy, then we will receive riches. The individuals who espouse this theory provide techniques such as using mantras and repeating positive statements to help a person make the changes necessary to get what he / she wants from life. However, when an individual truly understands consciousness, then that individual recognizes that the ego truth might not be in alignment with the beliefs operating at the unconscious Self level. The mantras are used to build ego defense. While ego defense is effective at earlier stages of ego development and can manifest our surface ego desires, for those wanting to move into Integrative Consciousness, defenses become blocks. In 1984, I regarded myself as an intelligent woman, yet life was reflecting back to me another belief system of mine that was unconscious, manifesting itself in the form of Brad and his views of women's limited value.

If my unconscious beliefs that surrounded this structure had remained unconscious and unchallenged, then life would have mirrored those dynamics also. The outcome of the computer project would have been much different, reflecting back failure instead of success because of my level of ego-development.

Summary of the Integrative Consciousness Process

In summary, external experiences that are appropriated to the ego can only be of a dual nature, an experience of bipolar opposites (Edinger, 1994, p. 13) based out of fear of the un-identified pole. An unevolved or immature ego can only perceive structures from the separating process, or as bipolar opposites, such as 'I am this, but I am not that,' or 'I am loving, but not hateful.' A bipolar aspect of a structure can only be a structure of the ego. Once the ego has appropriated the structure, then the structure cannot be absorbed by the larger state of consciousness and developed into the stillness of mind.

The larger state of consciousness can only absorb the structure when the polar opposites obtain unity, when you have identified your relationship to both structures. If you are reactive, then you have not integrated into the larger consciousness state the ego structure because it continues to be a defensive aspect of ego. When the bipolar opposites come together in the process that Jung calls the coniunctio, or the simultaneous experience of the opposites, then the larger state of consciousness absorbs the complete structure, resulting in Integrative Consciousness. This, then, is a state in which one interacts with one's environment from a feeling of connectivity and wholeness, without reacting to a polar opposite and identifying with the more ego enhancing structure.

Integrative Consciousness assumes the quality of the ego-defended structure and leaves in its place a quality of the Divine nature, that is, a unified structure based upon love.

Chapter 6

Development of Duality in the Ego

For there is nothing either good or bad, but thinking makes it so.

William Shakespeare, Hamlet

The Purpose of Separation

Separation serves a purpose of creating a strong ego identity or a means to begin the understanding of self. People begin to create an identity of self by seeing what they are not through separation. When the self has an identity that is mostly of positive attributes then a strong, cohesive, core begins to develop that will serve in later stages of growth when ego strength is important as a stabilizing influence in the Integrative Consciousness process. It is during integration that the individual's task becomes to bring together all the aspects he / she has separated from. It is having the awareness of this relationship to the projected or separated material or objects that provides feedback as to where we are in the integration process. The more unconditional love exists, the less judgment, the less fear in the relationship to those projected qualities, the less anxiety and the further along we are to integrating the totality of this quality within our own psyches.

The Separation Process during Childhood

Opposites or duality structures develop and the separation process occurs soon after birth when the child begins to see the mother / caregiver as separate from the self. The child then begins the process of identification, identifying with the good aspects of the mother and disowning the rest: 'I am this. I am not that. I am kind. I am not unkind. I am caring. I am not uncaring.'

The young ego needs to see itself as mostly good. This process strengthens the ego, so that at later stages of ego development successful integration of the disowned material can occur. The disowned aspects are what Jung calls shadow material (1966, 16: para. 451).

Initially, the child identifies with the good qualities of the mother or primary caregiver, and represses the negative aspects of the mother, or else projects them onto other people or objects. Thus begins the establishment of a cohesive sense of self that supports later post-ego development. Identifying with more good aspects of the mother establishes the self as something definite and positive, allowing the child a secure image of self, along with ego strength. The greater the secure sense of self, the more cohesive the self-image. Then, at a later stage in life, the easier it is for the individual to release attachments and integrate the opposites into the larger state of consciousness. The child with a weakened ego—meaning an ego that builds an identity from mostly negative mental models—will have less ability to take the psychic risks necessary at a later stage of development in order to break through the ego's defenses.

The child's quality of relationship or attachment to the mother also determines how well the child can create an internal image of security within him / herself. When the child recognizes more good qualities in the mother, he or she begins to construct a positive external image of the mother. Often the child may project that image onto an object, such as a favorite blanket, and thus the term 'security blanket'. Eventually, the child withdraws the image from the mother or the object that he or she has projected upon, and establishes an internal image of support and security. This allows the child a more secure sense of self, which helps him or her to venture into the world.

The child that has a negative image of the mother does not have an image of security and support. Therefore, this child withdraws this image of the mother and internalizes insecurity.

As a result, such a child has difficulty developing independence and venturing out into the world.

A securely attached child is more apt to take risks as an adult, a quality that assists the adult in facing the tasks of post-ego development into Integrative Consciousness. One has to be able to risk the security of the ego defense in order to venture into the vastness of the unknown, larger aspects of consciousness.

Duality Exemplified

To demonstrate the development of a duality structure, let us use the characteristics of kindness versus meanness. A newborn identifies with the nurturing, kind nature of the mother. As the ego develops, the child will see her / himself as kind as this is a quality he / she has defined as good, but will separate the self from meanness. The child's ego has created a bipolar structure that includes kindness, out of fear of the opposite expression, meanness. Again, this separation process occurs in order to allow ego development and provides the individual with a means to understand who they are. This separation serves in strengthening the ego and provides the foundation for consciousness development later when the Self is ready to begin this process.

However, as this person develops into adulthood, other people receive mixed messages from this person's outward show of warmness, because fear lies at the base of his or her kindness, whether on a conscious or an unconscious level. Thus, other people perceive that person's behaviors as inauthentic as the behaviors are arising out of fear of being mean and the need to be seen as warm and good.

As the person further moves into post-ego development, he or she may become more aware of his or her reaction to unkind people, which may initiate exploration into what this means. At times, this person might recognize unkindness within him / herself. These are two extremes of the ego expressing and both extremes are horrifying in their nature to the ego because, at the nature of this structure lies fear. As the individual begins to experience and accept the fear that underlies his / her kindness process, then he or she begins to provide the space needed in his / her consciousness that will allow the integration of the separated structure of kindness and meanness to be absorbed into the larger state of consciousness. This is the beginning of wisdom.

Integration Exemplified

After such integration, kindness and meanness in others causes no reactivity within the person's own psyche, only a profound understanding based on compassion and acceptance. He or she understands and accepts the fear that another has with either being kind or being mean due to his / her own experience of the vulnerability underneath the expression. The person has claimed a part of his / her psyche—meanness— that he / she has projected out into the external world, and transformed the fear that underlies this projected part into unconditional love.

As this person develops consciously, he or she reacts less to situations and people in the external world. The overall quality of this person's experience in general increases, and is not dependent on any external event. This person does not feel like a victim, nor does this person victimize others. The person feels he or she has a choice and owns power within a situation or a relationship. In contrast, when no integration of the fear-based ego structures into the larger consciousness takes place, then there is an internal conflict. This type of discord within an individual creates emotional distress and difficulties that lead to dysfunction within the individual. A conflicted and distressed individual develops greater ego defenses, and the internal strife plays out in relationships and external situations.

When a child is young, these defensive structures serve a purpose, allowing that child to survive fear- and anxiety-provoking situations, such as when mothers and fathers express their anger, or permitting the child to confront new situations or the emotional hurt that naturally results from life's experiences. If the defensive structures were not in place during these earlier developmental stages, then we would simply become an ineffective, blubbering mess when confronted with difficult or anxiety-provoking situations. For the young ego, projecting this disowned material is necessary if sanity is to exist and self-worth is to develop. However, if the young ego has internalized more bad than good aspects, this will result in the child's engaging in outrageous behaviors, destructive relationships, impulsiveness, emotional instability, self-harm, or in the worst cases, mental illness and insanity. At the later stages of development, these defense mechanisms become maladaptive, and it takes more energy to keep the defensive structure in place in order to protect the ego's sense of self and safety.

Many people remain at this stage of ego development. It is the 2 percent of people who begin to develop their egos through the process of Integrative Consciousness. If further ego development is to occur in adulthood, then the adult must encounter the disowned material through close relationships with others, and eventually within the self. As one continues through the process of Integrative Consciousness, he or she will enter the stage of integrating the opposites. Integrating the opposites means understanding and being present with the fear that underlies the separation process to begin with. An individual with a weakened ego does not have the capacity to merge the projected material, nor the ego strength needed to bring about the union of the opposites. Therefore, the ego continues to project the disowned material out into the world onto objects and other people.

When life situations challenge the ego in the post-ego developmental stage to drop its defenses and begin the consciousness process, our success in doing so is determined by the strength of our ego. Ego strength is not to be confused with a highly defended ego. A strong ego is permeable, open to learning, has a highly regarded self-image, and is not so easily threatened that it invokes the ego's defensive structures. Ego strength is determined by how highly developed is our self-esteem. How many of the attributes that comprise our self-image do we see in a positive light? How defined is our self-image by qualities characterized as strength and power? This ego strength will later support the stripping away of our defenses so that we can stand toe-to-toe with our disowned material and the fear within. Paradoxically, it is our allowing this vulnerability with the disowned material at a stage that initiates Integrative Consciousness.

The next step toward Integrative Consciousness is to bring about a union of the disowned material into a cohesive self. The result is then a more unified sense of self that has resilience, flexibility, and choice of action (not reaction) to every situation.

Jung understood that 'what is', or what we see as 'real' in the external world, is actually a projection of our ego, and that the quality of our relationship to those projections as well as our ability to not defend determines how far along in the Integrative Consciousness Process we are. If there is judgment or strong emotional attachment or reactivity to a projection, then we have identified with a pole and have moved into ego defense. It is through our evolving consciously that we begin to see our experience as it is and not through our projection onto a situation. In other words, the acceptance of our experience becomes wisdom. We see the truth in our reality that underlies all actions.

So how can we bring the quality of wisdom and knowledge through awareness, as well as acceptance of our dualist nature into our relationships, especially our marital relationships? Unfortunately, such integration does not happen without suffering. This is the reason most of us choose not to proceed, but rather revert to earlier stages, continuing in the separation of opposites to avoid pain. The key to the Integrative Consciousness process is exploring how we presently relate in the world, to situations, to others, especially in marriage or intimacy.

The Psychology of Opposite George

An episode of the television show Seinfeld deals with the polarization of opposites. The character George Constanza develops his life-success strategy, which he coins, 'the Constanza Maneuver' (David, 1994)–that is, living out the opposite of who he feels he is at an instinctual level. George is selfish, lazy, unfocused, and not confident, whereas 'Opposite George' is motivated, giving, and sure of himself. George understands that whatever his instinct tells him to do in a situation always ends in failure.

Applying the Constanza Maneuver, George sees a situation and understands that his response comes from an instinctual level. He then pauses and asks, 'What would be the opposite thing to do?' and acts in this opposite way, and achieves success. For instance, George feels insecure in his ability to attract a woman because he is short, bald, and has no job. He will not even approach a woman for a date, or else he creates elaborate lies about who he is. All of these behaviors ultimately result in his rejection. 'Opposite George', however, strolls over to a woman and confidently tells her that he has no job and lives at home with his parents, and then asks her out, resulting in a date.

In actuality, this could be an interesting practice of mental imagery—to take on the opposite pole of what we identify with, and present this quality to the external world as our self-image. When a projected quality or ego-attached image expresses itself in our life, the polar opposite also exists within our consciousness, and therefore is accessible for us to experience. For example, if we see ourselves as hard working, then laziness also exists within us. Perhaps our hard-working persona is in defense to our fear of being lazy and what being lazy would mean in our life.

If we go deeper into our fear of being lazy, then a basic fear of annihilation may arise. Our 'taking on' laziness would get us in touch with many fears that our hard-working persona masks. Some of those fears could be the need for others' approval, or survival fears that 'if I am not a hard-working person, I cannot survive in the world.'

In George's case, however, his motivation for experiencing the opposite is to gain success. George has identified with the negative-inspected structures for so long that his ego is weak and ineffectual. George's thought that he will become successful by doing the opposite springs from actions he has taken previously, based on his 'instinctual' self always ending up being unsuccessful. He uses the Constanza Maneuver to build an ego defense against his feeling insignificant or a failure.

At George's level of development, his experience had always been in living from a victimized perspective. 'I'm too bald, too fat, have no job, and I live with my parents. How could I attract a woman?' So experiencing the polar opposites begins to give him a sense of power and significance, which is crucial at his stage of ego development. George is actually building ego strength before entering into the later stages of ego development or, as in the myth of Inanna, gaining courage to knock on the door to the underworld of our consciousness.

Although George's motivation continues to serve the ego, experienced from another motivation—such as in service of developing Integrative Consciousness, George will want to feel his vulnerability. The experience of vulnerability would prove invaluable to the strong ego for it is an essential step in growth at a later stage of ego development, Integrative Consciousness. When one goes with awareness into feeling the opposite pole and into one's vulnerability of that experience, this serves to develop ego strength, not ego defense. Moving into vulnerability sends a message to the ego: 'I will not continue to be manipulated by fear; I will take on my fear, be present with it, and see where this takes me with this structure.'

Staying with the vulnerability from an expanded awareness allows the ego to expand large enough to carry the suffering that underlies our vulnerability, and not defend against it. It is only with a defenseless ego that Integrative Consciousness occurs. Many times when integration occurs, the pattern ceases, or does not result in suffering.

As you begin to understand our subconscious dynamics and the vastness of the subconscious, you may begin to explore the question of free will. It appears that free will is more than the will of our egos, and that these complicated unconscious processes do affect the choices we make that on the surface appear to issue from conscious free will. The chapter regarding relationships will further illustrate the extent to which free will is actually involved in choosing partners.

Summary

In summary, the framework that provides the foundation of Integrative Consciousness has at its base several fundamental principles:

1. Interpersonal relationships, both early in life and later in adulthood as we become aware of pattern and projection, play a central role in developing Integrative Consciousness. Interpersonal relationships become the road map, showing us where we are in our development.
2. An expanded permeable ego allows an objective experience or an opening to awareness of the self and of these interpersonal relationships, and promotes the development of the process of integration
3. The second component of Integrative Consciousness is acceptance of the self that is vulnerable and caught with ego defense. We become aware of this vulnerability as the defense expresses itself through projection of the duality structure. Heart-Centered awareness, which I will discuss later in the

book, helps to support this conscious witness state.

4. As the ego integrates more and more into the larger consciousness, the ego becomes Integrative Consciousness. Integrative Consciousness expresses the true essence of qualities such as free will, generosity, integrity to name a few. Then the individual is able to carry consciously more and more suffering, their own and another's. True service to humanity is born through this resonance.

So again, awareness, acceptance, integration, and resonance allow us to attain the path of Integrative Consciousness, and to live it in relation to others.

Reflective Exercise

1. Identify a structure that you have separated from yourself. An easy way of doing this is to complete the sentence, 'I am a _____ person.' The opposite of your adjective is the pole you have separated.

2. Now, take on the opposite by closing your eyes and allowing your mind to see yourself as the opposite characteristic. Use the meditative audio guide on the web page, **www.melissalowe.com** to assist you with centering. Remember to never do vulnerability work without centering or otherwise you may re-victimize yourself and actually build ego-defense. When thought appears to take you out of vulner- ability to the experience, acknowledge the thought and then return to the image of the opposite. After picturing this imagery, write down your experience as well as the thoughts that came in to take you away from the imagery. This recording of what transpired will give you insight as to how your ego reaches for the illusion of power. For example, I once sat with my vulnerability of feeling insignificant, as this was coming up for me during my day in the form of people saying

how important I was to them as their therapist as I felt an attachment to these comments (taking on the opposite here also). As I stayed present with insignificance, this took me to feeling incapable, which took me to feeling not being able to support myself and I would be homeless. The thought of my having an education would take me out of my experience. 'How could I have a Doctorate and be incapable and therefore I don't have to worry about annihilation? I must be done with this structure as I feel quiet now.' My having an education or a strong intellect is a defense that my ego uses when I am vulnerable, and it gives me an illusion of power. It took me out of my being present with this vulnerability. I was able to catch my ego at play here and returned my awareness to feeling insignificant. I wanted to loosen up my attachment to feeling significant to my clients.

3. Take note of the thought you had that pulled you out of the vulnerability. This is the defensive structure you use when reaching for power when you are vulnerable. Seeing the defense as it plays out in your daily life will help you to recognize when you are vulnerable in the future.

4. Write about an experience you had that was difficult and anxiety provoking, such as my experience with the microcomputer project. Describe the people involved. Write down a few characteristics you see within each person. Now, write about the difficulties you might have experienced with these people. Such as Brad reflected back to me my fear of not being capable enough to do the work, i.e. not smart enough, not prepared enough. He also reflected back to me my own belief structures I had of women and their abilities that were not beliefs I had on a conscious or intellectual level. If you had difficulty surrounding a project or an aspect of your career, then write what made this hard for you. Write about how you handled or related to the situation, or to the people involved.

Chapter 7

Awareness and the Witness State

If you touch one thing with deep awareness, you touch everything.

Thich Nhat Hanh

Awareness and the Witness / Observer State

Awareness is the ability to observe one's body, mind, and emotional response to life as it is expressed. Life presents itself on a moment-by-moment basis, and a person who is aware has the ability to understand the associated motivations that underlie his / her reactions or behaviors. The function of observation is much like that of a monitoring system that operates at the conscious level, witnessing life and its unfolding as well as the self's relationship with this unfolding. Only an evolved ego can allow a witness perspective to operate and keep watch on the ego's reactivity. An even more evolved ego allows the witness state to observe every moment of the day without the ego getting caught and reacting to fear. Very few individuals, less than two percent, reach this level of awareness (Joy, 1997). The chapter on acceptance discusses the heart-centering technique in detail as a way of shifting one's awareness into the observer state of consciousness, or the witness state, and allowing a level of complete acceptance for the situation that arises. Heart-centering allows a person to accomplish two of the elements of Integrative Consciousness, awareness and acceptance.

The Reactive Defended Ego's Evolution

An individual operating from an ordinary conscious state, or in a consensus reality state (a state of consciousness from which the majority of people function), typically is reactive and responds at different levels of reactivity from the almost unnoticeable to the extreme outward expression of fear and rage. This individual is in ego defense with whatever is occurring in a given situation. An individual who is reactive throughout the day has no access to the observer state of consciousness. When we have experienced the witness state and at times continue to react and remain unconscious to the dynamics underlying this reaction, then that means the witness, or observer, state of consciousness is receding from our awareness. We are very much in ego defense at this moment.

Defensive structures of the ego may allow an individual to continue to function within a certain set of circumstances, but then, as he / she begins to evolve into post-ego development states of consciousness, these defensive structures are released to allow Integrative Consciousness to occur. Many individuals have not reached a point of ego maturity that would allow them to have conscious access to the witness state. Those individuals, who operate from ego defense, have identified their egos to their thoughts, self-images, and emotions and hold an attachment to these structures. For these people, the ego defense structures are necessary to survive and function in their daily experiences, becoming so rigid that they cannot access the observer state.

Stage One: Emotional Reactivity

Let us explore ego defense with an example related to a recent political issue. This example has been organized in stages, but these are not hard and fast stages that one will experience as one begins the process of awareness. I have devised these steps to demonstrate easily a possible evolution scenario of the ego's development of awareness.

Imagine you are watching the late-night news, and you hear that Congress has approved the bailout for the auto industry. If you are operating from an unconscious state, you will just react. For instance, you may yell and scream at the television that members of Congress are idiots. The expression of anger gives you a sense of power. Anger is a primitive defense the ego appropriates so as not to experience feeling powerlessness. Anger erupts pumping up the ego and inflating it with power. You feel justified in your reactivity, and maybe you continue to harbor these feelings until your ego is once again able to repress them. You do not reflect on why you may be responding in this manner. You blame the industry and government for the nation's situation, and you feel justified in assigning guilt to these institutions. In this state of consciousness, your anger gives you an illusion of power; this emotion is a defense that your ego goes to in order to protect you from feeling a deep sense of powerlessness.

In contrast, as you advance in your ability to be conscious, then the observer state functions by first separating itself from the defensive ego self. So when you hear the news of the bailout, you become aware that your body is beginning to tighten, and that you are responding with emotional anger. You have the ability to perceive your first thoughts, which might be: 'Why is the government assisting the auto industry, when it is apparent that the auto executives have not managed their business? Other smaller businesses would not be permitted government assistance. Where is my bailout?' You may even be alert to how powerless you feel about this issue. You may even judge that you are not a good person to be so angry, creating more defense with your judgment on your anger with the situation. At this moment, you are observing without restricting the emotional response of anger or censoring your thoughts. You are conscious of a strong reactivity you may have with this situation, and you may also judge that you are responding to it. This is the first stage of becoming aware, that is, noticing when you are reactive to a perceived threat and fear but at the same time continuing to react.

Stage 2: Conscious Observance and Insight to Reactivity

This first stage may evolve to the second stage, in which you witness your reactivity but also become mindful of your growing acceptance of your reactive emotions of powerlessness and fear. Returning to the example above, you are conscious that you are responding with anger to the automotive industries' bailout, yet you also recognize that you are caught in your intense thoughts and emotions or ego defense. Therefore, you allow the reactivity to surface without censoring those feelings. You understand that such a response is part of your process of becoming conscious. You may even begin to see this reaction as an attempt to defend against a deeper feeling of powerlessness. This second stage may then develop into an ability to be present in the moment as you interact with people, situations, and objects. Your relationship to the external has begun to shift, becoming less and less reactive.

When the ego is experiencing powerlessness, it typically will reach for power, oftentimes in an expression of anger, as this provides the ego a quick and false sense of control. At this second stage, you may recognize that you are actually responding to a perceived threat or a past object relationship. As with many aspects within your psyche, such a response signals that you have not evolved past your reactivity with this one particular dynamic. You can discern your reactivity, initially with judgment, and then later the judgment falls away as the acceptance of your powerlessness grows.

For example, a past object relationship may be an experience you had with your father, when he had to use the family resources to help your wayward sibling until there was no money left for your college tuition. The way you initially perceived this situation as a young person could influence the way you react now as a mature adult to the current government bailout. In other words, you project the past onto the present, your father onto the government, your sibling onto the auto industry. But if you have the insight of pattern, this perspective can assist you in maintaining the observer state of consciousness without judging onto the projected object, the objects in this case being the auto industry and the government. Eckhart Tolle identifies this stage as coming into 'Presence' (2005, p. 165).

Stage 3: Integrative Consciousness

The second phase of witnessing your reactivity without judging it, can evolve into the third stage, which is Integrative Consciousness. That is to say, a person experiences awareness that is nonreactive, and it operates along with a true acceptance of and compassion for what is. The ego does not reach for defense, as it does not feel threatened or powerless by the situation, therefore resulting in no internal conflict with the situation. Some masters of this state of consciousness say that individuals can develop it to the point where even if they find themselves faced with a situation resulting in possible death, they feel only complete acceptance, for no real threat to the ego exists.

So, returning to the above example of the automotive industries' bailout, from an Integrative Consciousness perspective, in this stage you feel no reactivity upon hearing the news of the government's offer of financial assistance to the car companies. You do not relate to this issue based on a past object relation. This also does not imply a detachment of the situation. Detachment is ego-defense structure and sometimes masquerades as presence or stillness of mind. Instead, you have compassion for the many aspects of this situation that might appear in your awareness. You respond with concern to the people around you and experience an understanding of the greed that exists in this situation, of the fear beneath the greed, of the fear that these circumstances might place the economy in jeopardy and have a detrimental effect on workers if part of an industry goes under. You feel compassion for people's fear of being unemployed, or for the broader fear that this failure will have a domino effect on other businesses. You recognize how these fears operate within humanity, and how they serve the community as well as the individuals involved. There is no ego-defense structure that separates you from the experience. There is only compassion, understanding, and insight. When this integration occurs, then the experience is absorbed, in the moment, into the larger consciousness state. There is no aftermath of repressed feeling about the situation that can later develop into a past object relation that can be projected onto the next screen. Suffering, therefore, is not created from the experience. It is what it is, in this case, an expression of our humanity and the times in which we find ourselves as a collective.

Compassion in Action

An integrative consciousness perspective does not mean that when a person feels compassion, he / she does not take any action. Compassion does not mean inactivity. In fact, the opposite is true. A person will take whatever measure is appropriate for a situation, because he / she is not responding from the reactive levels of consciousness. The action a person engages in from this state may look the same as the action he / she engages in from other states of consciousness, such as writing a letter to a congressperson, but the motivation behind the action is clear: it is compassionate, with no underlying basis of fear and no attachment to the outcome. This action is co-creating with the structure. It is not reflecting back the fear that exists or expressing that fear in way of 'activity'. When a person's behavior comes out of this perspective, or this stage of consciousness, it will have a tremendous influence that the ego alone cannot perceive. For action taken from this Integrative Consciousness state understands the dynamics involved in the situation at larger systemic levels.

113

The Observer State as Ego Defense

One of the traps the ego sets up is that it uses the observer state of awareness to create the illusion that a person has integrated his / her consciousness. The ego cleverly employs what may seem to be the observer state as a defensive structure when in fact the person is detached. A person caught up in this ego defense can seem very enlightened, have access to all sorts of insightful thoughts, and be void of reactive emotions. Yet, when an individual is in defense, no matter what form it may take, he / she will not move into Integrative Consciousness because ego-defended structures do not integrate into the larger state of awareness. The key is to be mindful of when one is reaching for defense.

A feedback system that I use is to be alert to when I am vulnerable and captured by fear in the moment. I know that in the next instant, my ego will reach for power. Having practiced these techniques for years, I can instantly recall my desire to integrate these dualistic structures. That desire alone will allow me to remain in my vulnerability, without any attachments that might cause me to remove myself from that state of sensitivity. I remain with my fear, allowing it to be. The integrative consciousness process will proceed with its own timing, as its manifestations are in relation to other dynamics that connect to events beyond my control or even out of range of my personal world. These structures consist of such forces as the collective consciousness.

Projection: A Tool for Increasing Awareness

Projection is a tool we can use extensively to observe the unconscious and perceive this separation process of dualistic structures occurring within us. Projection enables us to catch our unconsciousness, for the unconscious is, well, unconscious and therefore not easily visible. Yet, understanding how to use projections, we can see easily what is hidden from us.

Projection is sometimes a defensive structure of the ego and is integral to awareness. It operates to protect the ego by 'projecting out onto our world' the aspects, characteristics, and dynamics that we cannot discern within ourselves, and the unidentified and identified poles, for such realization would otherwise be destructive to the vulnerable ego. If we could imagine the world as a blank screen onto which we 'project' our mind (both conscious and unconscious), then we receive insight into our mind and can be conscious of the very subject our ego is defensive about. And if we understand our relationships to the objects that we have cast onto that screen, then we gain still more insight into our unconsciousness. This relationship, specifically the *quality of relationship*, provides feedback to us as to where we are in the integration process. The less reactive we are to those objects on our screen, the less defense exists and the more readied the structure is for integration.

Our ego defenses are the blocks to experiencing Integrative Consciousness. Projection plays an important role in our attaining awareness, which in turn leads to Integrative Consciousness as we develop the quality of those projected relationships. Through our ability to observe our projections and then our relationship to those projections, we possess awareness, a key element in the Integrative Consciousness process. If a person can recognize these projections, then he / she is able to identify the duality structure in which his / her ego is engaged.

Balancing on the Balance Beam of Opposites

Jung states that the ego maintains its integrity only if it does not identify with one pole or the other of the opposites. If one is mindful of the opposites, then one is able to hold both of them in awareness at once without the ego reaching for defense. This is the task of a mature ego (Jung, 1916/1969, par. 425). This holding of both opposites is key to integrating the opposites into the larger state of consciousness.

If we accept Jung's premise that everything in the external world is a projection of our unconscious mind, then it is our observing the relationships of those projections that will give us insight as to where we are in the task of integrating wholeness within our consciousness. When there is great fear with the structure we are projecting, integration will not occur. Let us use the example of the qualities of diligence and laziness. You see an able-bodied man standing on a street corner begging for money for food. You judge this man as lazy, and you feel justified as you drive past, maybe offering the man money or not. You have projected laziness (i.e., this man) onto your screen. This sort of defense allows you to feel better about your relationship to homelessness or to a person having to beg and to your action of driving by him. If you can be aware that you have just made a judgment, then this gives you the information that you have projected an unconscious fear onto this man, who in our example is in the form of 'laziness'. Now you would examine your relationship with laziness. What does laziness mean for you? In the moments in your life when you have been lazy, were you trying to avoid something? What are your concepts regarding being lazy? Does society hold esteem for the opposite, which is hard-working individuals? Are you looking for social acceptance in working diligently? Is there any fear associated when you allow yourself to experience the feeling of being lazy? If there is, what is that fear all about? How do you feel about possibly being homeless?

When we begin to explore an unconscious operation such as our projections, we send an important message to the ego that we are not being fooled by our defense mechanisms, and that we are preparing to carry our subconscious fears consciously. We are ready to hold the defense and the fear simultaneously. This ability becomes an important step in Integrative Consciousness. As we begin to get in touch with our fears and stay present with them on a conscious level, we expand the ego state, and the ego becomes permeable enough to allow the important and final stage of Integrative Consciousness, that is, the absorption of the ego structure into the larger consciousness state.

In the case of laziness, you might get in touch with the fear of not being safe in the world: If you are not out there making it happen through work, then you might be homeless and on the streets, trying to survive. So your fear of not being able to sustain yourself underlies most of your actions regarding your 'busyness'. You operate daily out of this basic fear. Diligence and laziness, when they manifest as polar opposites, have at their essence the same fear. Fear is at the root and is the cause of separation. For example, in the case of the bipolar of diligence and laziness, both can be manifestations of the fear of failure. We work hard in order to avoid feeling like a failure, and we are lazy in order to avoid feeling a failure if we attempt to do something and it does not turn out. Our relationship with the opposites determines where we are in the Integrative Consciousness process. By being present with this fear, by holding it in the space of the mind, we can begin to discern where we stand in regard to the opposites. The greater the fear the more the separation and judgment toward that separated projection.

When we react to a pattern that we have projected out into the world, then the projection becomes feedback: we have separated the structure into its duality form. We have created opposites. We have identified with one polarity that 'feeds' the ego and defended against the other. This structure, because of its duality form and our ego-defense that is associated with it, cannot integrate into our largest consciousness state. The ego has actually appropriated the structure, and thus it becomes defense.

Multiple Dimensional Selves and the Development of Pattern

One way of looking at the development of dualism and the construction of pattern is to see the psyche as containing multiple selves, or multiple states of mind, that are arrested at certain stages of development or that contain strong patterns of ego defense. These selves carry out many and diverse activities and act upon their environment. We all have many selves, such as the part of us that totally enjoys 'zoning out in front of the television', the aspect of us that finds enjoyment in a particular high-energy, high-stress project at work, the part that enjoys risky hobbies, the side of us that is able to take a complex class in bio-physics, and then the part of us that is unable to put two sentences together that make any sense. At times when one represses an aspect of one's personality, then the repressed aspect expresses itself in more obvious and dramatic ways. An example that Joy discusses is that of Sadie, who, if she wants to be a 'good' girl and has defined her sexuality as 'bad', represses her sexuality (Joy, 1997). The repressed energy will gather strength and may eventually manifest itself in a much darker aspect of sexuality, such as dressing provocatively and having sex with many men, as the now Sexy Sadie takes on the full expression of this energy.

Multiplicity also serves to assist a person in experiencing life and all of its challenges. For example, Brugh Joy (1997) also would refer to his 'Super Doc' aspect of self. This aspect of Brugh had the capacity to engage illness and death during Brugh's tenure as a physician. This aspect of self provided Brugh with the ability to detach from his emotions. Brugh would refer to this aspect as his 'saving grace' as it was Super Doc that allowed him to perform his job without emotionally breaking down.

These parts, or 'states of mind' or selves, are defined as the total pattern of the brain's activation and its response to a particular moment in time and to a specific event. This state of mind is responsible for perceptual bias, emotional response, memory processes, mental models and behavioral responses. By focusing on our perceptions, feelings, thoughts, attitudes, beliefs, and desires, and how these elements are reflected in our relation-ships, we have the ability to discern the patterning, or to see the self, as it presents itself to our environment.

The Secret Life of Sam: Developing and Expressing a Defensive Pattern into Adulthood

As an example of a defensive self, or an ego structure, developing over time into an established pattern of relating, we will follow the experience of Sam, a seven-year-old boy when our story begins. This child experiences neglect from a mother who is never home, and on occasion the mother leaves the house after a domestic fight with the boy's father. Sam interprets his mother's failure to look after him as, 'I am worthless and unlovable, and people / mother will abandon me.' After daily experiences of his mother going away for long hours, Sam reinforces this feeling of worthlessness. He interprets, and may be right, that his mother wants to leave her husband or, in Sam's mind, the family. Then, in the future, whenever Sam encounters an experience of 'mother' going out for the evening, he may interpret this event from this earlier pattern of abandonment, which reinforces the pattern. In physiological terms, he is developing neural pathways in the brain that, when stimulated by similar triggers, will fire certain neurosynapses and release emotional and behavioral patterns to this stimulus or trigger. The activation of this state of consciousness can become a personality trait. As Sam's state of mind becomes clustered into a specialized self, then this becomes an enduring state of mind that repeats this pattern across time and can generalize the trigger (Siegel, 1999, p. 231-57).

Later in life, as an adult, Sam may even generalize the pattern, so that he might interpret even an unreturned phone call from a woman as complete rejection. Sam will react from this abandonment pattern with an unreasonable level of response: that of the seven-year-old child self. This child self of rejection has an established set of brain neuron activity that fires along a set path, stimulating the same neurons in the same order and producing the same reactions. This abandonment pattern, or mental model, can be looked at as a separate self within this individual that 'takes over' this person's conscious state, or brain functions, if you will, and perceives the most innocent of behaviors as rejection and abandonment. Sam is developing a pattern of relating to an object (the abandoning mother as object) which he generalizes into adulthood, as we will see. It is reasonable to say that part of Sam's development was arrested at this seven-year-old stage.

The selves that comprise who we are can stop maturing at certain stages in our processes of growth. In our example above, Sam's cycle of neglect and abandonment occurred at age seven, so this self may have the responses of a seven-year-old even when Sam reaches age 30. Let us look further at this example to illustrate how these multiple selves develop and can play out later in life.

Sam, now age 10, lives with his parents. The child may be picking up on his mother's desire to leave the marriage. Sam, with his established 'I'm worthless and mother leaves' pattern now interprets his mother's dissatisfaction with marital life as her wanting to withdraw from him. The boy, in an effort to have some control in the situation and defend against his strong feelings of unworthiness, then tries to be the best son, doing all the chores, even those he is not asked to do, and extending himself out so that his mother does not feel any stress when she comes home from work. Sam, in his efforts, is trying to exert some power over his mother's emotional state in the hope that she will not get angry and withdraw from the family, or even worse, withdraw from him. However, although the child goes out of his way like this, his mother does choose to leave and Sam's father ends up raising him. The son represses his anger at his mother, burying it deep within his subconscious.

Expressing an Object Relations Pattern as an Adult

Sam, as a grown man, suffers many rejections from women. He has the type of romantic relationships that normally occur in human experience and that normally end, such as a few dates and then the other person moves on. But Sam regards each ending as a complete rejection of who he is, and each ending gets him closer to that feeling of being abandoned. He feels he is not good enough and can never be good enough for a woman to stay and not leave. Sam is angry, but is unable to express his anger, as this will be seen as his being a 'bad boy' that will push the woman / mother away. He has to be the good boy in order to be loved.

Sam eventually finds himself in a relationship with a woman, and very early in the relationship he offers to help her with some plumbing in her home. He extends himself out in many ways to help this woman, just like he did as a boy with his mother. He has the underlying motivation that if he is good enough, she will not leave. Sam is acting out of unconsciousness. He is not aware of this wounding pattern, nor of how he sets this experience up. After dating for one month, the woman decides not to see Sam anymore.

Sam interprets the woman's moving on as a complete abandonment of himself. He has given so much to this relationship, and yet it is not adequate. He feels rage that has not been expressed before, rage that he could not show to the mother and to the previous women he dated. Sam, in a dark fury, strikes out against this woman, beating her. When he finally realizes what has just happened, he is astounded that he could have done this to a woman. He considers himself to be a caring and loving person. In terms of Integrative Consciousness, Sam's behavior lacks authenticity, as it has evolved from unresolved conflicts within the self-states of consciousness. The woman is shocked at the unexpectedness of this behavior from a man that had been so wonderful to her before. Sam is now serving time in prison.

Patterns arise because we continue to project out into our external reality a structure in order to defend our ego. Through this strategy, we attempt to avoid pain and suffering time and time again. The example of Sam's fear of abandonment and how that is a motivating factor in his generosity and assistance to the women he dates illustrates that this fear began operating in Sam at age 10, once his mother left the family. This abandonment pattern then surfaces and generalizes in his relationships with parents, spouse, boss, or anyone he regards as a significant person in his life. His fear of being left may be projected out into many forms, such as alcohol abuse, the avoidance of relationships, difficulty relating to many people, and so forth. Eventually, when the timing is right, Sam will begin to be aware of his projection, which usually takes the form of meeting women who leave him, until finally he sees himself as the common denominator in those relationships. It becomes important, then, for Sam to have a specific healing process that will assist him in integrating his selves with these specific fears across time.

Sam's Pattern Expressed in Light of Integrative Consciousness

When we look at this example and consider it as if Sam has developed his ego to the state of Integrative Consciousness, then the following would have occurred as a natural progression.

First, awareness would come to Sam after several failed relationships in which he tried to give the woman everything she needed based on his unconscious fear that she would reject him. The key point to remember is that fear motivates Sam, and that the ego defends against the anguish of rejection by trying to manipulate the woman into staying with him. Initially, this process occurs at unconscious levels. Sam tries to influence the woman and situation by giving of himself so that the woman will not leave. Therefore, the ego sets up the illusion of control through the structure of, 'If I become important to the woman /

mother, then she will not leave.' An aware Sam notices that his defenses against abandonment begin not to work effectively. Women continue to leave no matter how good he is to them. He experiences more suffering. He may also notice that he is the common denominator in this scenario of his life.

So at first, he may continue to react in the same way as before, but what is now different is the awareness that occurs at the same time. He may become conscious of his underlying emotions and structures, such as the rage he has toward the woman, for she is the object of his weakness, of how easy it is for him to give her his power, and she reflects his vulnerability. He may begin to perceive his anger toward himself because he is weak in relationship with women, and because he allows women to 'take advantage' of him. His fury gives him the illusion of power and control. The rage is invigorating. If his ego is not expanded and strong, then the ego cannot allow the vulnerability of rejection to be carried consciously. The ego must defend through the defense structures of his pattern and through the illusion of power that accompanies rage.

But let us say, for the sake of proceeding on toward Presence or Integrative Consciousness, Sam has had prior experiences of developing a strong self-image and ego strength. As discussed earlier, ego strength signifies an open, flexible, permeable ego and not a highly defended ego. So now Sam has a strong ego developed through his constructing a positive self-image, either through a great career or in other ways, such as receiving positive feedback from others. Sam may have a cognitive under-standing of his pattern with his mother because in experiencing another failed relationship he may have asked himself, 'When did I feel this way at other times?' His answer came to him in an image of his cleaning the house as a boy to make his mother happy, and the mother leaving the family (him) that evening just the same. In Sam's case, maybe more than an intellectual under-standing is needed to have a pattern fall away. He begins to have the awareness that perhaps his fear of rejection is his Achilles heel. Possibly his experiences of women who reject him and of relationships that always end are meant to open him up to experience abandonment and have a *knowledge* of this structure at a deep emotional and intellectual level.

The Different Paths of Evolving Through Insight

There are many different ways Sam could approach this insight of abandonment. One path is to allow life to introduce opportunities for him to 'take on' his fear consciously by allowing him to feel his vulnerability to abandonment in the moment each experience occurs. While in a relationship with a woman, he must have awareness as the fear comes up, preferably in the same instant, and watch as the ego defends. In Sam's case, he would see himself doing things for the woman that he really does not want to do, but that he does in order for her to love him and not leave. Eventually, the goal is for a person to get to a place where no rationalization, intellectualization, denial or ego-defense of any kind exists. As Sam stays present with the abandonment, the compassion for self, and the acceptance that he is as he is—fearful of abandonment, he may witness himself having anxiety when the threat of abandonment presents itself, such as seeing his girlfriend on the phone. He tunes in to his anxiety and may even experience a shift in perception, realizing that his girlfriend is only on the phone speaking with someone and that this behavior is not related to a future event of her leaving him. His anxiousness then melts away, and he has found liberation from this pattern.

This level of acceptance would mean that Sam now comprehends that rejection / abandonment is an element of his relationships. When a person reaches this level of understanding, then the ego is carrying the suffering of abandonment without defense. Once the ego can put down its defenses, then a person experiences suffering in the moment and is quickly released from it, without this feeling being transferred into anxiety / fear and stored in the recesses of the body / mind system. Awareness becomes the way we can carry our own suffering, suffering that is rightfully ours to bear instead of placing it outside of ourselves in the form of projections and repeating patterns. With awareness comes the end of our perpetrating on others the actions we sometimes take as we project our suffering and fears out onto our world.

If Sam had not moved into Integrative Consciousness, he could have defended against the fear of abandonment and attempts, as in the past, to manipulate it. When the ego is vulnerable and powerless, it will attempt to reach for control unless we stop and become present with the pain, holding it in our awareness until some shift in perception occurs. Sam can now begin to assist his woman out of the pure pleasure of giving to her and not through manipulative behavior devised to avoid the fear of rejection. The former is authentic behavior because the action is in alignment with the motivation.

Chapter 8

Relationships: The Path to Awareness

Once the realization is accepted that even between the closest human beings infinite distances continue to exist, a wonderful living side-by-side can grow up, if they succeed in loving the distance between them, which makes it possible for each to see the other whole against the sky.

Rainer Maria Rilke, Letters to a Young Poet

Projection and Patterning in Intimate and Marital Relationships

Intimate relationships are one of the more powerful arenas through which we can further awareness into the unconscious by understanding projection, because we have a propensity to work to improve these relationships. The expression 'blinded by love' aptly describes the initial process of the coming together of a man and a woman. At first, we project onto our partner our unconscious ideas of 'all man' or 'all woman' attributes. Our partner actually may carry the essence of these qualities unrealized within him- or herself. Nonetheless, we find those traits lacking within ourselves. For instance, if we feel unconfident, even though we may mask it with a confident air, then we are more apt to project the quality of confidence onto our partner. Of course, our partner is unlikely to live up to our unconscious, high expectations in the long run. Eventually, he or she must and will fail in our eyes, and such failure begins the process of Integrative Consciousness within our psyche.

If we ignore our partner's inability to meet our expectations and continue to criticize or repress our feelings regarding our unmet needs, then we remain unconscious to these dynamics within us. It takes a tremendous commitment to do the soul searching necessary to move beyond our projections. The process of consciousness becomes even more difficult when we are in denial that anything we see within our partner has anything to do with our own psyche.

Typically, a man projects soulful love onto a woman, meaning that men look for the internal feminine within themselves, such as inspiration, unconditional love, acceptance, nurturing, and passion. Women, in contrast, generally project empowerment onto their male partner, searching for the internal masculine that feels power, the ability to manifest goal-oriented behaviors, approval, and the capacity to be outwardly active and creative in the material world. Until men and women are able to recover these qualities within themselves, they will live out the puer / puella relationship, that is, son to mother, daughter to father. As a rule, it takes a person's commitment to a marriage, an engagement, or a live-in partnership in order to initiate the process of moving toward consciousness through an intimate relationship.

Initially, we may be attracted to someone of the opposite sex as a way to play out our projected inner male or female. (For same-sex relationships, the person is actually looking for the internal same-sex attributes within him- or herself.) When we decide to explore such a relationship with this person, every-thing appears to be right in the world. We feel warm, excited, loved, and all the other emotions that accompany the initial stages of a relationship. We have fully entered into the uncon-scious, and yet we have gone there unconsciously.

The Illusion of Wholeness

In intimate relationships, on an unconscious level, women constellate their unconscious male, or father figure, while men constellate their female, or mother figure. We feel complete when we are with the other person. The famous line from the movie

Jerry Maguire, 'You complete me,' applies here (Brooks, 1996). This line strikes at the heart of all romantics. It conjures up thoughts of togetherness until 'death do us part' and a sense of wholeness. This feeling is the result of what is occurring on an unconscious level, as it is projected onto our partner, and what is taking place on a conscious level within us. Together, the unconscious projected aspect and the conscious aspect become the ego's perception of wholeness.

We create this semblance of completeness as long as we continue to project our disowned material onto our partner— 'This plus that', or 'You plus me equals one'. The illusion of wholeness is the seduction that our ego creates, and our ego is fine in going along with this plan because typically it feels so good. What we do not understand is that our feeling that we are complete *depends on our partner carrying our projection.*

In addition, we generally misunderstand that, while in this moment, the positive aspects that are projected onto our partner and that bring us together are the very thing that will push us apart as we begin the awakening process. The separation occurs because the positive aspect becomes a quality we perceive negatively in our partner. As we awaken and can begin to take back our projected aspects, we start to move in the direction of 'One plus the other equals more than one.' In conscious relating, the relationship of the couple is greater than both individuals.

Phase I: The Birth of Conscious Relating

One of the first stories that depicts this process is that of Adam and Eve, and Eve's sin of taking a bite of the 'the forbidden fruit'. This act brought on God's banishment of Adam and Eve from the Garden of Eden, sending them out into the world of suffering and responsibility. When we begin the awakening process, we too enter the world of suffering, awareness, and the discovery that we are vulnerable in our nakedness.

Let us use the example of competence. The woman observes

competence within the man, and she is attracted to him and adores this attribute. This projection is usually a positive attribute of her father and how her father provided for her. For his part, the man is drawn to the woman's adoration, and to the way she makes him feel secure. This projection is a positive attribute he desired or maybe received from his mother. The woman in this case is projecting her unrealized inner masculine, or one aspect of that masculine—competence —onto the man. The man is projecting his inner feminine, or one aspect—his desire for acceptance and love—onto the woman. When they are together, they feel happy and complete, not realizing that their projections are qualities they have not yet recognized within themselves and, initially, not fully actualized in their partner.

Yet when one of the partners begins the awakening process, that is, takes the bite of the forbidden fruit, he or she begins to see the opposite of the projected quality in his or her partner. Perhaps the husband is anxious about an important meeting at work. Perhaps when he is at home, he asks his wife how to operate the television remote control. Perhaps he is not decisive regarding a family problem. The wife then begins to feel critical because her husband is no longer carrying the positive quality she has projected onto him. She starts to express her criticism and withdraws her admiration and love. The husband feels unloved as a result, and perceives his wife as controlling and critical. The couple has redefined the relationship through their negative or dark projections at this stage of relating. They have left the Garden of Eden.

The Initial Attempt to Transcend the Parental Psyche

Each of us has the task of transcending both the conscious and unconscious parental influences. How well we are able to accomplish this task predicts how well we will be able to avoid projecting those relationship dynamics onto our partner. In other words, this is the formula for how successful we will be at consciously relating. In our culture, this challenge of transcending the parental psyche typically begins in the late teens.

We can gain a great deal of insight into ourselves if we explore what was going on in our life at the time we became involved in a serious relationship or marriage. What qualities did you perceive in your partner that you admired? What aspects did you not like?

If you reflect on a time in your life when you were ready to leave your parents' house and the security they afforded, you can also discern a great deal. Think of the moment when you stepped out into the unknown world with the task of supporting yourself. What did you do when faced with a new situation? How did your ego defend against the fear or threat of the unknown? If you attended college through the financial support you received from parents, government loans, scholarships, or other monies, then this does not count. Instead, explore the time after college when you became self-supporting. It is during this period that you would have established a pattern of how you would approach new experiences in your life.

The pattern activates and becomes established during this time, and will repeat itself later in life when one encounters similar situations. This pattern also arises when the process of Integrative Consciousness occurs, as the ego has to give up power and control and release itself into the vastness of consciousness, which the ego views as an unknown entity. How well you complete this initiation task of leaving the parental home lays the foundation for how well you address the task in relationships, as you typically then tackle and transform parental relationships in a committed intimate relationship.

Here is an example from my own story of a pattern in operation when one is preparing to step out into the world. At the age of 21, I was a senior in college. During my college years, I had a goal, which was to be a psychologist. This image supported me through all the challenges of school, work, and the many situations in which I found myself as an adventurous young woman.

The summer of that same year, I looked on the bulletin board in the psychology department and realized that students graduating with degrees in psychology were earning salaries of $6,000 a year. I was making more money working in a department store as a clerk! My heart stopped. Fear overtook me. Knowing that I had less than a year left in college and that I needed to support myself, I panicked. I stumbled out of the psychology building and into the computer technology building, and signed up for computer classes, determined to have a strong minor in computer technology, a rising field at the time, before the invention of microcomputers.

Within the same instant of my looking at the job listings, my dream of becoming a psychologist was destroyed. For the first time, fear overtook my desire and passion for psychology. Along with my dream, I also lost the zeal and excitement I had for life, and became overwhelmingly in touch with insecurity. This was the first time I understood the power an image (such as my psychologist) has to give us resilience, strength, and courage to face the challenges that life will bring.

Within three weeks, I had developed a severe and painful case of shingles, and a wise medical doctor informed me that I was 'stressed-out' with school, my social life, and my workload. He told me that my skin was my first defense against the outside world, and that my skin, the largest organ of my body, was 'sick'. Being young, I told him that he was incorrect, as I had the same schedule I had had for the last three years. Nothing was different.

Resource Image as Means to Anchor State of Consciousness

I was wrong. Something had changed: the internal image of the psychologist that had previously sustained me now no longer did so. I had lost the ability to see the happenings in my life from the perspective of 'the psychologist'. This state of consciousness was not swayed by fear of the unknown. She was focused, determined and driven by passion. She was present in the here and now. I resorted to searching externally for my support system. I found it about a week later in the form of my future husband. I saw him as intelligent, confident, and as a man who could accomplish anything he set his mind to. I had projected onto him the protector image of my father. I had transferred the internal protector image of the psychologist to someone outside of myself. We became engaged within two months, and then all was right in my world. The skin disease healed.

Exploring this time as I look back on it, I am able discern a pattern that when I feel insecure, I look outside of myself for assistance. At a time of crisis, it is difficult for me to go within and reflect on my experience. I find it challenging to discover the solution within myself. The problem with finding one's strength in the form of another person is that then one's support system resides beyond one's control. In my case at this time, my future husband became my tower of strength. But if that person leaves, so does the comfort and assistance one desires. Therefore, one becomes greatly attached to that other person, and the need to have him or her around develops into codependent behavior. It is not wrong to have aid and help from another person in a relationship. However, the key is not to *need* support from that person, especially when one moves into Integrative Consciousness development.

When we have the ability to integrate consciously, the result is an internal wholeness and completeness that is not an illusion of support (typically an image within women), or of love and acceptance (typically an image within men), and therefore we do not seek after it in the external world. From a state of Integrative Consciousness, one feels the assistance or love internally in the moment, and reflects that sense of love and help to the outer world.

Ego consciousness is based on illusion, or a reflection of the real thing, whereas Integrative Consciousness does not depend on the actions of another, that is, an object or an external event to obtain that feeling of wholeness. When the internal image of support is intact and / or we are consciously integrated, then we are able to experience support, intimacy, and reliance on another human being without forging a codependent, ego-attached dynamic.

When we begin to live with this type of awareness and bring it into our relationships with our partner, government, church, or corporation, then we perceive the world and its current events from a different perspective, not from that of victim.

Stages of Integrative Consciousness through Relationship

Phase I. Emergence of Consciousness — Emergence of the Opposites Stage

Returning to our relationship process, let us look at this process in stages. The initial phase of the Emergence of the Opposites is the projection onto our partner of our unconscious attributes that we desire to own within ourselves. This is a romantic stage, one filled with feelings and dreams that the world is beautiful, and that we are loved. We embrace the other and feel satisfied. In fact, we are unconscious at this stage. The greater the ego threat and fear then, the stronger the feeling of love. How well our partner carries our unconscious dynamics determines the depth of our love.

The emergence of the opposites arises out of our desire or our hatred for an object. In the case of an intimate relationship, it typically begins with desire for the other. This is what brings us together with our opposite. We must keep in mind that an intimate relationship does not necessarily have to be with

133

another person. It can also be with a career. Actors or athletes will project the opposites onto their careers and, therefore, strongly desire recognition that they are the best in their field. The decision to be in relationship with an object is a decision that usually is outwardly attractive.

Bargain Stage

As the emergence of the opposites constellates in the other or is projected onto our partner, the bargain is set. Our unconscious orchestrates these processes by luring the ego in order to avoid fear, and entices the ego into the later developmental process of Integrative Consciousness. One such bargain is, 'If you love me, then I will always be happy,' or 'If I am a successful actor, then I will be happy.' It is a necessary seduction, and we are willing participants. However, the bargain sets us up for the betrayal phase, which comes when we begin to realize we are not getting the results we hoped to obtain through the deal we have made. It is important to understand that, typically, we unknowingly make these pacts.

When one enters a sacred contract such as a marriage, then the contract / marriage provides a container for the exploration of the psyche and the process of Integrative Consciousness. The marriage is the opportunity to face the disowned material and the bargains we have made, and open into the Integrative Consciousness process. Any dynamic, such as a disowned projection, will not support the Integrative Consciousness process, as it is of ego defense (Almaas, 1986, p. 135). Defense frequently appears as a negative projection onto our partners, or in childlike relationship patterns. It is important to keep in mind that when the ego is defended with a structure, it is unable to integrate into the larger consciousness state (Almaas, 1986, p. 135).

For example, let us say you discover your partner has not been honest or forthcoming with you about something. You are outraged, and vigorously point your finger at your partner, never really looking at your own faulty relationship with integrity. Perhaps you often sense that everyone around you is lying. Could you need them to be honest because their dishonesty makes you feel unsafe, or maybe because you too have suspicions about your own integrity? Again, your safety is dependent on the actions of someone outside of you. The bargain then, is, 'If you are honest with me so that I know everything that is going on, then I can feel safe and will love you.'

Betrayal and Disillusionment Stage

As we move into the betrayal stage in a relationship, we may begin to realize that the life or the bond we have with another person is not what we bargained for. We may be married and it may be a good marriage, but we may notice that we are lacking something in our life. We are not really happy. We begin to reflect upon the pact that we set up during the initial phase of the relationship. Whatever deal we made, it is not now giving us the happiness we wanted, independent of whether or not we achieved the bargain or got what we wanted when we entered the relationship. We discover that what we thought life was about is not really so, and we feel disillusioned.

Many of us have difficulty moving beyond this stage. So we repeat this entire process by once again projecting onto another person those positive attributes, allowing the seduction to occur, and making a different agreement. This new compact might take the form of starting a new job, or beginning a new love relationship, or even finding within the old partner new positive qualities to project and balance out the negative. These are efforts to mask the suffering we experience within the old pattern. Terminating the previous process of integration and beginning again with the seduction, or building up ego defense is easier than continuing to move forward. It becomes too painful to enter into the next phase, Descent into the Unconscious, and many people repeat Phase I over and over.

Phase II. Conscious Descent into the Unconscious—The Realization Stage

The realization stage is the time to search for answers. In this stage, priorities change—what we thought was important does not seem so important now. We begin to connect our wounding patterns, and realize how they continue to manifest from our childhood and into adulthood. This is the time when we confront the task of leaving behind our parental psyche and taking on the mantle of adulthood, becoming responsible for our own lives. The masculine aspect of our psyche recedes as we begin to discover that our world does not operate by manipulating external objects and people, an attribute of the immature masculine. Surrendering our masculine is difficult, as the masculine is how we got our needs met in the past, such as taking action in the outer world when we felt some anxiety. The action we take during this stage is not outward but rather inward action, as we begin to get in touch with thoughts, emotions, and images that arise as we face circumstances in our lives. It is during this stage that we also commit to remain conscious.

Once we have completed these tasks—uncovering wounded patterns, identifying the projective disowned material, leaving behind the parental psyche, and surrendering the masculine—then we are ready for the next phase, Integration.

Phase III. Integration

Here, we begin to build inner trust by overcoming life challenges with a different approach. We nurture ourselves by seeing how we have wronged ourselves, and begin to experience loving forgiveness for ourselves, knowing that we are involved in awakening. This phase puts us in contact with both our inner masculine (for women) and our inner feminine (for men). The inner masculine and inner feminine at this stage are developed and mature in the power they contain.

At this point, we also begin the important task of balancing the polarities of our consciousness by recognizing our projections, and working to accept these projections totally as our own disowned material. During this stage, we open up to the creativity of new ideas. We begin to maintain inner quiet while doubts surface, when faced with disapproval from others, and while we lose our identity, that is, who we thought we were. This is the final ego structure to release in the Integrative Consciousness process.

It is by being vulnerable to these processes that integration soon begins. Vulnerability is not to be confused with weakness. Vulnerability, with the desire to grow consciously, takes on the purity of the attribute. Pure vulnerability is about being open. When we remain vulnerable, the ego is not defended, nor does it reach for power. Vulnerability means being present with our fears as they surface. We recognize these fears by understanding our projections and patterns without defense. We accept what occurs in the moment. This constitutes surrendering. If we are vulnerable, then we have the courage and real strength to be present with our undefended ego.

As we complete each of these tasks, the duality constructs that brought us into this process begin to transform, and our larger state of consciousness absorbs these structures. When we are able to hold both dual dynamics in our awareness at the same time with an open, vulnerable heart, then Integrative Consciousness takes place. Our ego is left with clarity and no need to defend against these dynamics in the future. Our ego becomes subservient to the larger state of consciousness and the process of integration.

As we can see, relationship is the initiation into the underworld and the realization of inner potential, as it is so rich in unconscious material ready to rise to awareness.

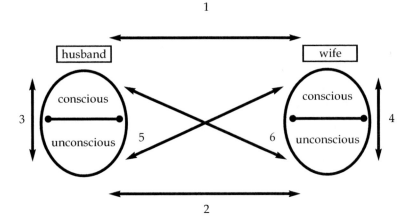

Figure 1. The marriage relationship expressed through conscious and unconscious relating.
Figure adapted from 'Transference and Countertransference, Perry, C. *The Cambridge Companion to Jung*, Eisendrath and Terence-Dawson. (1997).

Relationship Dynamics of Partnership

One of the more striking bits of information that I have encountered in my study of relationship dynamics is the understanding that as I project onto my partner or another person, he or she has access to my subconscious dynamics via the path of my projection. When this realization hit home for me, I understood how vulnerable we are in our relationships. Using a diagram from Jung (1929, 16: p. 222) and adapted by Perry (1997, p. 147), let us explore exactly what I am describing here.

In Figure 1, the following points indicate the marital relationship between partners. Line 1 is the conscious relationship between a man and a woman. This is the external relationship taken at face value. Line 2 is the unconscious relationship between partners, or the projective qualities that are occurring unconsciously. Line 3 is the man's relationship with his unconscious material, and, respectively, Line 4 represents the woman's. The next two lines are what give each party access to the other's unconscious material. Line 5 is the wife's need for her husband's ego, that is, her unconscious projections onto her husband, and through that projection, the husband has access to her subconscious material. Line 6 depicts this relationship for the husband.

What Jung (1929, 16: p. 222) describes through our unconscious projections (line 2) is the means by which we give another individual access to our unconscious material (lines 5 and 6). Have you ever wondered how your partner seemed to know that you were insecure about something, and how he or she could use that in an argument to attack you? Another example might be when you are fighting with someone and want to hurt him or her. You might make wounding remarks and wonder why you said them. The more aware we are of our unconscious material, as depicted in lines 3 and 4, then the less someone can manipulate our subconscious material in relating to us.

An example of this dynamic can be illustrated by the case of a friend who is a health practitioner and his patients. Even though this example is not a husband-and-wife relationship, one can apply this dynamic to any relationship type. The practitioner, Joe, has a pattern of feeling powerless and insecure about his ability as a doctor, and he needs approval from women. He is not conscious of these patterns that operate within him. He may for the most part think he is a good practitioner, and he actually is an effective doctor. Yet, within him there is a deeply rooted unconscious struggle of not being 'good' enough.

One of the behaviors he uses to defend against this feeling of powerlessness and insecurity, especially when he first meets a female patient, is behaving flirtatiously. Women patients typically are receptive to this flirtation, as it makes them feel special and cared for by their doctor. His sessions with these women contain intimate closeness and are therapeutic, in his assessment. One of Joe's female patients enjoyed these flirtations until Joe planned to give up his practice and move across the country. She felt rejected, and complained to Joe's supervisor about his behavior. The supervisor then fired Joe for what she saw as unethical practice.

He now faces the loss of his job and the accompanying humiliation, which reinforces the part of him that believes he is not a good practitioner. This is, then, another subconscious dynamic, his outer identity masking a deep-seated belief that he is not the 'good doctor'.

Actually, knowing I give others access to my subconscious through my own projective material, motivates me to do the inner work of Integrative Consciousness. I would like to avoid the dramas and situations that may come up, especially in relationships in which power and control are a strong pattern of relating. I must keep in mind that when I provide 'the hook' through my projection, this allows another person access to my subconscious fears. Even one's projection onto a stranger gives him or her access to one's subconscious material.

Catching Projection and Patterning Through Communications

In 1993, a colleague of mine, Laurie Schmidt, and I took on the challenge of reducing many projective aspects to their elemental fear. For example, the need for approval and fear of disapproval can be reduced to fear of abandonment / unloved. What we discovered are two elemental patterns—fear of abandonment / unlove and fear of no control / no safety. In our therapy sessions and group work with couples, we began to observe that even what appeared as the most innocent of conversations between a couple that were having difficulty in their relationship, contained elements of ego defenses, projections and patterning.

Take for example the following conversation between husband and wife:

H: Hi Honey, I'm home.

W: Hi, Jim.

H: If it is okay with you I am going to play poker with the boys on Thursday night.

W: Oh, really…Well, Okay.

H: What's wrong with you?

W: Nothing is wrong. I'll find something else to do. You just have a good time.

H: I'm going to watch the game (escapes).

W: (tears welling up.) Sighs. Okay.

In the above conversation, the couple appears to not be using much verbal communication. There is a tension underlying the conversation. Now let us look at the same conversation below in the dysfunctional relating table, with the cognitive and feeling processes and the subconscious patterning that anchors a certain perspective within the individual. Observe how this couple is not communicating consciously. While not much is being

Dysfunctional Relating
Control vs abandonment

Verbal	Cognitive Process	Feeling Process	Subconscious Patterning
H: Hi Honey, I'm home. W: Hi, Jim.			
H: If it is okay with you I am going to play poker with the boys on Thursday night.	I know she is going to be upset and angry.	I feel angry. I feel like I'm 10 years old and have to ask permission. It is as if she is Mom.	Controlled by Mother/authority
W: Oh, really…Well, Okay.	Why would he rather be with someone else instead of me?	I feel scared. He may have fun without me and then leave me.	If I'm good enough Dad/Men will not leave.
H: What's wrong with you?	I knew she would act like this.	I am sooo angry. I feel smothered	Control/ No control.
W: Nothing is wrong. I'll find something else to do. You just have a good time.	Why can't he stay at home with his family. I do.	I am anxious. He does not love me or he would be here with me.	Abandonment/ Security.
H: I'm going to watch the game (escapes).	I'd better leave or this may become a fight.	Escalated anger, frustration of feeling cornered. Avoidance of Mother/anger.	
W: (tears welling up.) Sighs. Okay.	Can't he tell I'm hurt and want to discuss this?	Hurt, fearful, rejected, abandoned.	

verbally said there is a great amount of activity going on at deeper levels. This communication is reflecting fear patterns of control within the man and abandonment within the woman. When we are unaware of what is going on within ourselves we are at risk at having miscommunication with others.

In the healthy relating table, let us observe the dialog between the couple who have clearer thoughts and calmer emotions. They are not activating past object relational patterns and this is reflected in the conversation between the couple. Almost the same words but the feeling tone is different and the messages they are sending are warmer.

Healthy Relating Verbal	Cognitive Process	Feeling Process	Subconscious Patterning
H: Hi Honey, I'm home. W: Hi, Jim.			
H: If it is okay with you I am going to play poker with the boys on Thursday night.	I enjoy playing cards with the guys. I have a good time with my friends.	I feel excited, lucky to have good friends.	Nurturing through many relationships.
W: Oh, great! Nothing is coming up or is planned.	I think it is great that Jim has good friends and nurtures those relationships.	Warm, happy feelings.	Nurturing through experience of Jim's happy excitement.
W: I think I will finish my painting that I am working on.	I enjoy painting and will now have alone time to work on it.	I feel peaceful.	Exploring creatively.
H: I can't wait to see the finished work.	My wife is talented and I like to see her happy.	I enjoy seeing her happy.	Unconditional support.

As you can see, the importance of becoming conscious of our patterns is directly related to the clarity of communication with our partners and people around us. The more we become aware of the deep forces that reside underneath then we cannot project these forces but we carry them. In our dysfunctional communication example above with the wife that is seeking security in her husband, the seeking has reached such a point that she fears she may lose him and her safety along with him. This fear results in manipulations and allowing herself to be biased in her perceptions of situations especially in regards to her husband. She is missing an opportunity to understand her deeper mystery and possible liberation from this particular fear. By the wife becoming conscious of her interrelationship with security / abandonment as it is being projected onto the screen of her husband she has the chance to turn her relationship into one of caring and intimacy. This can also be said for the husband's shadow. When we are unaware of the shadow operating within us, then we become frightened and will cast out onto others our reactivity with the shadow. This reaction takes the form of anger, judgment and other negative emotions.

Chapter 9

Power and Control in Relationships

Whatever you fight, you strengthen, and what you resist, persists.
Eckhart Tolle, A New Earth

When one confronts the challenge of going beyond the ego and into an Integrative Consciousness, he / she faces a preeminent state of an un-evolved ego. The ego's goal is to obtain a sense of power and to preserve the organism. It is when part of our psyche is rendered powerless with fear that the ego strives to regain its strength through power-grabbing and control struggles in relationships. Ego-based power is a false sense of power, as it is comes from manipulating the outer world. As long as we can exert this sort of control occurs, then we feel powerful. This dynamic is very subtle and seductive, as it leads us believe that we are in the present moment and are not involved with a projective process, such as perceiving the situation from a dualistic structure of our mind by which we have identified with one pole.

As discussed in the previous chapter, an individual in the initial stages of a relationship will project onto his /her partner positive attributes, as well as the resolutions to his / her defensive patterns. The thought 'You complete me,' while romantic, actually truly represents the projective quality of each partner as he / she transfers positive or resolving qualities onto the other. The two become one. For example, a woman becomes involved with and marries a man who she sees as intelligent, hard working and with a good job, who makes sound decisions and uses good judgment. She views him as her protector or a father replacement. He is the solution to her fear of being unsafe in life, and to her inability to find the protector within herself. She feels protected as long as the man continues to carry her protector projection.

The man also projects positive attributes onto the woman. For instance, he sees her as supportive, loving, caring and attentive. He considers her as his supporter, someone who regards him as important and powerful. Again, this perception completes his self-image as a man. All is right in the world as long as each person has the other at his / her side. Yet neither one realizes that their love is ego-derived and based on the other's ability to fulfill their projections and needs. The woman loves and supports her man as long as he continues to carry her positive protector image, and the man believes she loves him because he is a good man and a protector.

You've Lost That Loving Feeling

Typically within a few short years, the relationship transitions from one of passion, excitement, and loving feelings to one of criticism, lack of communication, and withdrawal from the other person. This phase occurs in every relationship that is on the verge of awakening to larger aspects of consciousness. What occurs next may vary from relationship to relationship. Using our example cited above, the woman, realizing her loss of love for her husband, may begin the process of building ego defense that will allow her to find a semblance of the love she initially felt. Another woman may continue to be critical, believing she must have made a mistake in regarding this man as a good provider. She will punish him for fooling her. In other words, this man will carry the sins of other past men in her life. If the current man is ready to play out this experience of punishment, and this fulfills him, then the relationship will continue and will serve these individuals. The relationship, though, will not bring the pair a sense of happiness or fulfillment.

In a case where these dynamics go on playing out, in the

example above of the couple engaging in punishment or criticism, then the tension needs to build for the individual(s). The strain and stress may increase until the relationship ends. Or else, if one partner or the other can make headway in the part he / she contributes to the relationship dynamic, then this usually initiates some type of awareness and can bring back the projection or understanding of the depth of the pattern. By seeing the projection and having awareness into the dynamic under- lying the need for this defense, begins to loosen the compulsion to act unconsciously and keeping the defensive structure in place. The result is more possible solutions and directions the relationship can travel.

In the example noted earlier, if the woman is able to be reflective, accountable, and ready for the next stage of ego devel- opment, she can grasp that she is critical of her husband. For instance, perhaps she witnesses his failure to take care of the plumbing problem. Or she recalls the time he lost several thousand dollars in a bad financial decision. Her regard for him as less than her ideal protector permeates the projected ideal that she had of him initially in their relationship. She begins to withdraw her approval of him, and she is openly critical. Yet, she begins to realize that maybe her criticalness is unfair.

The husband senses her distance from him and begins to see his loving and approving wife as nagging, critical, and controlling, as less and less his supporter. Beneath the surface level of their relating, the wife's subconscious is challenging the projected image of her father-protector pattern onto the husband. This idealized image of her father is an unreasonable one for her husband to live up to. Once her husband fails to hold the idealized projection, the wife withdraws her approval and replaces it with criticism.

The husband, who has relied on the wife's support in order to feel good about his self-image and to assist him in facing challenges, begins to see her as judgmental and controlling, which is his pattern of relating to his mother. If he has not developed a strong sense of self—perhaps through his career endeavors and through who he is as a man without the wife's projection—then he feels devastated by the withdrawal of her positive projection onto him.

When a relationship reaches these critical stages, the couple enters into the danger area, attempting to reach for increased domination and control within the relationship by becoming manipulative and hurtful to each other. Each one is at the mercy of his / her own unconsciousness. The reach for power is due to his / her own insecurities and to the partner not holding the positive projection. The two individuals feel vulnerable within themselves and within the couple relationship. Their egos feel insecure and powerless as a result of the rejecting and manipulating interactions, and they attempt to manipulate each other, trying desperately to push the other person into becoming what they are unable to find within themselves.

Usually to remain in one's vulnerability within a relationship is difficult to do unless the two individual(s) have an understanding of the deeper process that is evolving within their consciousness. This is not about the relationship or the other but about each individual's inner dynamics that he / she projects onto the relationship and their partner. Each person feels betrayed, blaming the other for not holding his / her positive projected attributes. The wife feels unsafe or unloved, and the husband feels unloved or weak as a man. Both of their egos will want to defend against these raw feelings of fear. The couple moves between the roles of feeling in power and then feeling powerless. They have entered into unconscious relating and into a power relationship, as each struggles to regain a sense of control. Both people are in ego defense and are relating to the other person's heavily defended ego.

Placing a Cog in the Wheel of Manipulation

The wheel of manipulation turns and the pain intensifies. Being stuck in this dynamic is a no-win situation. Often, each person ups the ante until the misery reaches the point at which the couple will either end the relationship or build up higher and higher ego defenses. If the fear of being alone is greater than the hurt in the marriage, the couple eventually builds a stronger ego defense against the fears each has currently projected onto the other, which means they will push their suffering down and stay in the marriage.

The need to enter into a new relationship or to find another means of escape is strong, as each partner wants to recover those loving feelings experienced in the beginning of their relationship, which is the sense that all is right in the world. Both people are caught up in parental patterns of relating to each other.

It takes an awareness of how this process is operating in the relationship to stop the cycle. The individual's psyche might be pushing toward opening up to the process of Integrative Consciousness: awareness, acceptance, and integration of his / her ego's defense structures. Integrative Consciousness results in bringing the duality structures, or the projections reflected in the relationship, into transcendent oneness. Very few people go on to this next stage, the stage of allowing their ego to 'take on' the fear that underlies the pattern.

For the Integrative Consciousness transformation to occur, one person must sacrifice the illusion of power, stay with his / her vulnerability, and be present with the fear until the ego begins to shift from a heavily defended and reactive state to a vulnerable, permeable ego state. Sacrifice is a key element of moving into acceptance and is discussed in the next chapter. A person must sacrifice the illusion of power that manipulation provides and stay in vulnerability. The next hurdle will be to stay with the awareness and acceptance of vulnerability underlying the defenses until integrative consciousness occurs. In some instances the pattern is finished, independent of integration occurring and the opportunity for integration is lost.

Bringing the Relationship into Conscious Relating

To grow out of this conflict and begin Integrative Consciousness, the woman must 'take on' her fear of not feeling safe in the world; the husband must 'take on' his fear of disapproval. By assuming the fear, each is admitting to his / her responsibility in promoting the conflict within the marriage. This willingness to acknowledge the fear also sends the message to the ego of their readiness to shoulder their subconscious fears. It also begins to loosen the attachment that one has with the conflict. In this example, the husband begins to break through his attachment of needing approval, the wife, her attachment of needing someone to make her feel safe.

These patterns have layer upon layer of fear attached to them. For example, the husband describe above may soon realize his anger and resentment toward his wife have roots in his rage at having to take responsibility for supporting his family financially when he was growing up. He may realize that his feelings stem from his reactions against society's demands that he be the provider for his family (demands that most men begin to experienced around the age of 18).

Gathering the Pieces of Your Scattered Psyche

Taking back the projection involves the willingness to feel vulnerable to one's fear and the ability to free one from their attachment. Then the ego realizes the defensive structure it has used in the past. The ego sees the defense for the illusion that it truly is. For example, the wife must withdraw her projection of the protector and understand that ultimately she is responsible for taking care of herself. She has to find the protector within. This may take her going into her fear of being out in the world alone, unprotected or unsupported. She begins to lose her attachment to needing someone to provide safety for her. This type of vulnerability work becomes easier when done from a focused heart-centered state of awareness, as will be discussed in the next chapter. Heart-centered awareness is a state of consciousness that is stable and that assists in containing the ego, so that the ego does not reach for defense against the vulnerability. We must remember, the larger consciousness state can only absorb the undefended, dual nature of ego (projected qualities), and this requires a person to be present with his / her vulnerability for as long as it takes to integrate.

In our example above, the wife must stay vulnerable for as long as she is able, or until the uncomfortable feelings shift from those of fear to compassion or acceptance. In her process, she may experience the surfacing of other fears, such as not being intelligent, not being skillful, or insecurities about whether she would be able to contribute to the workplace, about her sense of value, about the possibility of her being homeless or even annihilated due to her helplessness. At that point, she must sit with each fear as it arises and shows its face—reflected in her judgment and projections of the world, people, and objects— until the defensive structures drop away and the fear transforms and integrates into the larger consciousness state.

Conscious Relating
When You Think You Are Aware . . .

Reclaiming the ego's disowned and defended material is a process filled with pitfalls the ego creates to take us out of the vulnerability. In order to keep us from feeling pain, the ego gives us defense mechanisms as an escape hatch. The ego wants to find defense and will manipulate in order to, once again, be comfortable. The ego can achieve this sort of pleasant existence, but it is tenuous and based on external situations, for it involves controlling situations around itself. The following is an example of how even insightful, intelligent people can be fooled into thinking that they have the ability to remove themselves from power dynamics. Even when watching for the engagement to power to occur, we can believe we avoided power when in fact, the ego's defense once again seduced us and caught us yet again.

Dancing Around Fear

During my doctoral studies, at a seminar discussing power and control, the professor structured a small group to explore power and control in relationship, and ways that we can remove ourselves from these dynamics. This becomes a very tricky endeavor because power is so seductive. We can believe that we are conscious, when actually we are caught in a power struggle, only we are the ones that have the power. This is not an expression of Integrative Consciousness.

Now by nature, this room full of doctorate students had a large amount of defended ego, along with a heightened insecurity, some of which stemmed from everyone wondering if they were as intelligent as the person sitting next to them. At the time of this seminar, I had experience in working with power and control in relationship, both as a therapist, as an employee, and as a wife desiring a more conscious relationship.

I perceived the anxiety in the group and within myself, and understood that when there is uneasiness the ego comes in with defense and reaches for power. Anxiety is one of the first signs to be aware of in order to catch the ego as it begins to set up a situation to grasp for power. One can gain much insight into the ego's patterns of defense by observing it in action when one is anxious. I knew from my own projection of feeling unintelligent the importance of being present with my own feelings, and so I sat in a heart-centered state of awareness with my own anxiety, willing to be present with my vulnerability without the need to change it. Up to this point in my life, I had had much practice in finding quiet through meditation. Even so, I was extremely nervous. The professor asked for a volunteer to talk about an experience in which he or she had felt vulnerable.

One woman stepped forward, and everyone in the group breathed a sigh of relief that they themselves could, for the moment, avoid the hot seat. The woman moved to the center of our circle and began discussing how she had been abused as a child, and how she had learned to perform so as to distract her abuser, in order to manipulate him as well as the situation. This 'performance' delayed the abuse, and she obtained some semblance of control over her situation. This was an important survival skill for her as a child, and served her extremely well.

As she shared her story, she had captivated our group. She referred to her ability to perform for this man as her being a 'Dancing Bear', a term she had coined. The group of insecure doctorate students was tearful and sympathetic.

I sat in wonderment at what was occurring within the group dynamics. I felt the power shift from the group—including the professor who, as the designated leader has the unchallenged power—to the woman, no easy feat. She was in control, owned the power, and received sympathy from all involved. The group was under the assumption that she was vulnerable. It was willing to give her this, as the students wanted to be distracted from their own vulnerabilities to their own fear. I continued to sit with my own fear and also the fear that I sensed from the group.

Before I narrate what occurred next, I want to examine my experience of being present with the fear that I sensed from my classmates. As I have stated, I perceived the anxiety I picked up from the other students as the insecurity of not being as intelligent as another when in a group of other doctoral students. Now this may or may not have been at the root of the uneasiness that others were experiencing. I might have been wrong about the cause of their nervousness—it might have been my projection onto the group of my own insecurity—but this does not matter. What is important is that my insight provided me a way to begin to connect to the group members' vulnerability. It allowed me a portal to step out of the power struggle. I do not see the other (in this case the group) as having power over me and therefore I can remain in my vulnerability.

As I fully connected to their vulnerability, then I stopped relating to the group out of a power dynamic. My seeing them as vulnerable helped me to stay present in my own vulnerability, and did not promote my reaching for power over them. Even if their insecurity was entirely my projection, I was attempting to remain present with an underlying fear. I viewed them as who they were: just as powerless as I. There was no need for me to possess power over them. When I was connected to their vulner-ability and to my own—meaning that I was present with my underlying fear and what I saw as theirs—then I was removed from the power struggle in the class setting. The chapter on resonance discusses this phenomenon more fully.

Now, back to the group exercise on power. The professor discussed the 'powerlessness' of the woman who had shared her vulnerability. I continued to sit with my own feeling of insignifi-cance in this group of intelligent people, sitting with what I sensed was the group's anxiety, as well as feeling compassion for Dancing Bear. Yet, I realized that the story she had shared, while filled with horror and pain, was a situation that she had rehearsed in front of a group before. She had attended counseling sessions for many years, something she had confirmed earlier to the group. This classroom setting was not a circumstance in which she was completely vulnerable, as the story's dynamics was conscious to her and she had reflected on it many times. The story was in the control of her ego. It was something of her past of which she had awareness.

To really help the students get in touch with vulnerability, it would have been more useful if the professor had asked each of us to reflect on our current anxiety and fear as we sat in the group, for there was a great deal of fidgeting and darting of eyes. To be aware of the here and now assists in getting beyond the ego's defenses. The subtle control emanating from this woman's ego on an unconscious level, the group's willingness to be seduced in order to avoid or be distracted from their own vulnerability as they felt sympathy (not to be confused with compassion) for Dancing Bear, all of this allowed the woman to assume power within the group.

The professor was captivated by the woman's story and her ability to be 'vulnerable' with the other participants. He was seduced by his ego's 'hook,' which he later confirmed as his need to promote his agenda that we, as a collective, experience vulnerability and understand power dynamics.

Standing Alone in the Collective

The professor then looked at me and remarked that I had not commented, as had the other students. I took a deep breath, knowing the risk I was about to take in confronting the collective's defense of power, and knowing my own psyche's need to differentiate from the anxious group. The ego cannot work in collective forces, it either becomes intoxicated or victimized through a scape-goating process, especially if one is carrying the shadow of the collective. I was carrying the group's shadow of remaining present with my vulnerability and what I assumed was the collective vulnerability. Could I remain present with my insecurity? The group also had a need to differentiate from me, as I was being present with my anxiety and my vulnerability. The group wanted to defend against theirs. I looked at the woman and said, 'You are still Dancing Bear performing.'

Then the other students turned their wrath onto me. How dare I criticize Dancing Bear! 'She at least has the courage to be vulnerable,' I heard someone say. I was flooded with a new set of fears. The fear of not being as intelligent as my classmates changed to the feeling of the rejection of the collective. I experienced the group's need to 'punish' me for daring to stray outside of the fold. They were exerting their power as the collective to bring me back into the fold and not to have me shine the light on the collective or the individual's darkness. Before the focus shifted to me, I had been holding the desire to move with my vulnerability. I had stayed with my insecurity, loosening my attachment to intelligence and acceptance, while most members of the group wanted only to be distracted from their fear. I was the outsider.

The group was now strongly trying to pull me into alignment with its identity and actually found an area I could not stay present with. As I suffered comment after comment, I stayed heart-centered and allowed my vulnerability to the group's rejection to wash over me. Then my suffering became too great for me to remain present. I succumbed to my fear of having the group's disapproval. I found it interesting that the group could listen to Dancing Bear, yet could not be open to my opinion.

The Subtle Art of Manipulation

The professor said that it was abominable for me to say this when I had not volunteered to be vulnerable in front of the group, and that Dancing Bear had taken that risk. With a slight smile, he then asked if I would allow myself to be vulnerable by sharing an experience. With that question, he had tossed the gauntlet into the center and all eyes were on me to see if I was ready for the challenge.

Ironically, in that moment, I was aware of placing myself as a target for potential attack from my classmates. I was fighting back the tears and knew that I was lost to my ego's fear. The group had found the exact button to push within me to get me to succumb to their power and they could remain in their comfort zone. And, I knew I was going to manipulate my surroundings and make the attempt to reach for power. All of this I was observing as I symbolically picked up the gauntlet and accepted the challenge by moving my chair into the center of the circle of waiting students.

And so, I sat crying and shared a wounded story of my own.

I shared a story of a disorder I have, dysphonetic, much similar to dyslexia but associated with verbal processing in the brain and the difficulty of pronouncing words. I watched in amazement as the group's earlier wrath now turned to sympathy, and I felt that surge of power a tangible sense as it moved from the group to me. And, again, I felt the wonderment that I was influencing the group. I felt in control, although from outer appearances, I was a victim and one to be sympathetic toward through the story I was sharing. Where just moments before, I was the recipient of the group's wrath, I now had their growing concern. Even Dancing Bear was sympathetic to my story and reached out to grab my hand. The group showed sympathy toward me, forgiving me of my earlier transgression, and some members even seeking me out during a break to talk with me.

From the moment of my speaking up regarding Dancing Bear's performance, I was aware of the wrath of the professor, Dancing Bear, and the group, and this became too much for me to carry consciously without my ego's defense. For while the story I shared made me vulnerable and painful in its sharing, I too had reflected much on my story and had appropriated some of that story's vulnerability to ego defense.

Thus, I too used the defense that had worked so well for Dancing Bear. Hey, if it worked for her it should work for me. Even though I had explained my statement regarding Dancing Bear, my attempt to exert power over the group was successful, seducing even the professor. It did feel good, although from my understanding of ego and the Integrated Consciousness process, it was an illusion of power. I had sacrificed a moment to hold something greater: the possible integration of this part of my ego and the attached structure into larger consciousness. I needed the group's approval more than I needed to sacrifice the illusion of power of the ego. To suffer from my classmates' criticism continued to be too great a fear for me—too great to allow me to remain present in the suffering.

Sympathy Versus Compassion

In that seminar, I quickly understood how feeling sympathy for an individual involves an attempt to have power over another's situation, as well as power over one's personal vulnerability to another's situation. There is a difference between sympathy and compassion for another. To have compassion is to take on other's suffering by holding it in the space of one's consciousness, as if it were one's own. Compassion does not mean gaining control over the structure. In contrast, sympathy involves ego separation and, therefore, ego defense. The group's attention, hugs, sympathetic tears continued through the break, and I felt good in the illusion.

If the professor wanted the group to experience vulnerability as an element of power in relationship, he would have been more successful if he had had us stay in the moment with a present vulnerability, such as my fear of not being as intelligent as the other doctoral students (I do not think I was alone in that fear). But the majority of the participants were not interested in becoming aware. If the group's goal—or the Group Self—actually desired to have a transpersonal experience to power, my only question would have been, 'What then would be the group's experience? How would they relate to me differently as I was being present with vulnerability?'

The professor failed to give us tools to be present in the moment with ego vulnerability. Without a process of holding the ego stable in order to have the ego become large enough to carry the suffering or to have a transpersonal state of consciousness come in to carry suffering, then it is better to have the defensive structure play out. The group's willingness to become distracted with Dancing Bear and my own experience demonstrated the students' unfamiliarity with Integrative Consciousness practices.

The ego is a very slippery creature. When one thinks he / she has broken through ego defense, another defensive structure takes its place, and one may be unconscious to this defense strategy. Von Franz, in her book *Projection and re-collection in*

Jungian psychology, has contributed much insight into the workings of the collective experience and a conscious relationship to the Self (Franz, 1980).

Grasping the Slippery Pig . . . er . . . Ego

The difficulty in doing this type of depth work lies in knowing when one is caught by ego defense. Ego defense is subtle and seductive. It feels better to have a sense of power that comes when we are seduced into thinking that we have all the answers, are justified in our actions and everyone is wrong. While this seduction of power can serve us at one stage of development, when one wants to develop into a present state of consciousness or enter into Integrative Consciousness, then power dynamics are ego defense and block the process.

I could have seduced myself into believing that I was vulnerable in my storytelling because the awareness that my ego had taken hold of the story I was telling was so subtle. I cried and shook while telling the story. I appeared vulnerable. Yet, I was aware I felt more powerless with the group's disapproval, and that I felt a surge of power coming from the group's sympathy in my telling of my story. Such a rush of power does not mean I had worked through a vulnerability. There is a difference between ego power, which is dependent on external circumstances, and the power of presence, in which the power is internal and not at the expense of another external object such as another person or in my case, having the group's sympathy.

The sense of control I experienced in this group experiment was the result and a condition of the response I received from an outer level. First, the change in the external environment occurred, and it determined my experience of a sense of power. With Integrative Consciousness, the power that arises when one is present with one's vulnerability comes from within first. It does not rely on what is happening in the outer world. The circumstances occurring in the external environment, in fact, have not changed when one feels that internal power. The ability to discern internal power arising out of a person's state of consciousness and power that occurs due to an external change in environment or situation is essential when working with ego defense structures. Once integration takes place, an integrative consciousness affects change in the external world through a person's just being in this state of consciousness.

Therefore, in my example, my feeling my fear of vulnerability to the group's disapproval gave me feedback that I was in ego defense. Eventually, a sense of quiet, an inner stillness would have entered, and my awareness of feeling powerless due to the group's disapproval would have disappeared, even though the class continued to express disapproval. When a person's sense of power is independent of outer events, then that person knows that he / she is in the Integrative Consciousness Process. This is power transformed, not dependent on another. The quality of this power is that of clarity of consciousness.

The Seduction of the Ego

How do you not allow the seduction of the ego, but instead become informed that you are caught in ego defense? First, it is necessary to become aware when you are vulnerable with a structure. When you feel the potential to be hurt, then the ego wants to step in and provide defenses. We know we are vulnerable when we begin to detect the subtle signs of anxiety, such as a tightness of the muscles, a clenching of the jaw, and eyes averting, to name a few examples. If we can remain in the moment with our vulnerability, without reaching for defense, then the ego expands and becomes large enough to bear the structure.

The longer we can carry our fear-based structure, the further we move down the path of consciousness. The heart-centering process works well, as the state of consciousness it induces gives us the ability to be present with the fear without going into ego defense.

Chapter 10

Acceptance

It is only with one's heart that one can see clearly. What is essential is invisible to the eye.

Antoine de Saint-Exupéry, The Little Prince

Acceptance is the second component in the Integrative Consciousness process and the element that most people involved in consciousness work do not attend to or address. The reason why many individuals fail to work on this aspect is that when the ego achieves awareness of a dynamic, it typically appropriates the dynamic and defense enters in the form of ego-inflation. So when a person identifies with a revelation, he / she has just become unconscious once again. In other words, that person has unwittingly found a means to feel better, more in power and more in control. Once individuals have reached some insight, it is usually during this time that they abort the process of Integrative Consciousness. They think they have it made, that they can deal with this issue, telling themselves, 'Okay, I have this one figured out. I will be fine when I encounter it again, because I am really quiet with this, and it really is the other person's thing.' Oftentimes, people believe they have moved forward with a dynamic, a duality, or a conflict structure into which they are awakening, when in fact they have moved it into a deeper defense structure.

Acceptance is the key to advance into integration; it allows the ego to be present with a structure in a state of vulnerability until integration occurs. We must remember that integration of the ego-owned, dual structure does not occur with ego defense in place. When a person has insight into the dynamic that is playing out on his / her life stage, then that person has to take steps to the next level, which is being present with the vulnerability. Awareness of the vulnerability assists a person in remaining on track with integration and makes it more difficult for the ego to move to defense. A person's ego will try to defend if that person is aware that he / she feels susceptible to hurt or harm. The challenge becomes how not to reach for that defense. The trick is learning to stay with the feeling of vulnerability until there is acceptance or integration. Jung (1916/1969) speaks of holding both of the dualities of the structure in one's consciousness at the same time as a means of assisting the structure in coming into wholeness. He asserts that wholeness is only possible if one remains conscious of both polarities at once.

For example, if a man observes criticalness in the women with whom he relates in powerful positions, such as a boss, wife, or mother, and he perceives a similar connection in more than one person or circumstance, then he has come upon and owns a piece in this projection. It is important for him to bring awareness to this projection and to the nature of his relationship with it. The way that he responds to this dynamic provides feedback as to where he is in the integration process. He is projecting his own fear of feminine power and the fear of not having acceptance and love. He can probably remember a time when the feminine became controlling and critical of him and he felt forced to succumb to her power. He might have become resistant to her authority, or felt rejected by the woman. The intensity of his anger or anxiety becomes a barometer as to how much defense he has with the projected dynamic, in this case feminine power and acceptance.

The more influence that the subject of projection has over you, whether in a boss-employee relationship or an intimate relationship, such as with a spouse, the more evidence you have that you are directly encountering such a dynamic. It is crucial to discover why you are projecting, start the practice of withdrawing the projection and begin to improve the quality of your connection to this dynamic. In the case of a lack of control, if you believe yourself to be independent and in control of your life, then you are probably struggling with fear of no control. In order to work with this process, you must hold independence alongside your fear of no control or need for power within the space of your mind, at the same time if possible. Eventually, you must hold the two polarities together at the very moment when this dynamic is being played out on your personal stage. This is why the characteristics of strength, courage, faith, sacrifice, compassion and allowing are important in this period of a person's development into acceptance.

The Resource of Heart-Centered, Observer Awareness

Another resource to employ in this phase is heart-centered awareness, which places an individual's state of consciousness in the witness, or observer, state, a powerful condition of the mind when he / she is engaged in vulnerability work. The witness state enables a person to look at a smaller aspect of the self from the viewpoint of an observer aspect of the self as he / she engages in an interaction. If the person has not developed an ability to observe in this way, then the difficulty of being present with vulnerability exists. The person will typically re-victimize him- or herself in the situation. As a result, he / she will create deeper suffering as well as a greater attachment to the pattern or defense that he / she habitually relies on to avoid vulnerability.

Heart-centering provides the key to dissolve out of ordinary, ego-driven conscious states into a state that inspires and imbues you with transcendental perspectives. You can see more clearly and more deeply your personal shadow and often times the purpose of this shadow to bring you into a greater development. Heart-centering allows you to see the inter-relationships of objects versus the polarizations of things.

Returning to our example of criticalness, if you have an

encounter with a boss whom you regard as critical and you are required to follow a decision from that boss, a decision you view as 'stupid', you might walk around feeling angry and defiant. You may not want to do the best job you can and may be fearful of the criticism you are expecting to receive, or you might take another path and just build up resentment. While it is possible for you to be in awareness that you are projecting, you are actually victimized by your projections, unable to begin the process of taking the projection back.

If you can instead enter into the observer state, then another aspect can take center stage within the mind. Heart-centered awareness can bring you into this state. Through the 'lens' of this observer aspect, you may witness the situation and your reactivity without experiencing the emotional depths of the victimization that often occurs when a person has not established the observer awareness. In other words, you do not feel resentment, fear, or anger in the victimizing fullness of these emotions. You understand that your boss is not completely critical. You recognize it is your difficulty with criticalness that is preventing you from addressing the situation with clarity. From the observer vantage point you can allow your emotions to play out, while at the same time there is a larger presence in your awareness that understands you are involved in a greater process than this projection on your boss. You are engaged in growing spiritually and psychologically, ready to release any attachments that you have with the critical feminine.

Heart-Centering as a Defensive Structure

As we discussed in the beginning of the previous chapter, where awareness can be turned into defense, so can a heart-centered state become defensive. It is so powerful a tool to remove a person from emotional suffering that he / she might wish to enter into this state to avoid feeling the depths of emotions related to a situation.

When your motivation is to dodge your emotional response to what is happening, then you have once again entered into defense. However, by tweaking your motivation so that you set the intention to enter into heart-centered awareness as a means to fully take on the dynamic and to remain in your vulnerability, then this state does not become a path of escape for you. Suffering serves a purpose to bring you into a greater development, remembering this allows you to not reach for the momentary relief but to stay the course.

Strength and Courage

A person needs courage and strength to stay the course when it appears that nothing he / she is doing is working out favorably. Let us return to the example of Dancing Bear. In this situation, I was feeling insecure about my ability to hold my own intellectually with the class of doctoral students, and I worried that they would see me as unfit to be in a graduate program. I was aware of both my own and the group's anxiety and the possible consequences that might come from presenting to the class what I saw as their, or the collective's, reaching for power and using Dancing Bear's distraction as a means to divert their attention from their own unease. While it did take courage for me to make this observation to the circle, my ability to have strength to hold the course within my own psyche by being present with my fear of collective disapproval proved too much, and my ego defended. As part of my defense, I used my classmates' sympathy to win their favor. My encounter with a group's disapproval would come another day, which it eventually did, playing out on a much larger and more important stage and in a far greater encounter with fear.

In the classroom, the group reacted to my nervousness and my initial intention to stay present with my vulnerability without defense. I had offered the hook for the other students, in the form of my needing to win the group's acceptance. The group used that hook to get me to succumb to the collective defense against the group's overall anxiety. The fear I felt when I did not obtain their approval proved too great for me to continue to be in my vulnerability.

Even if you are aware of the underlying dynamics of a situation, if you feel uneasiness and are not centered with your awareness, then another person with whom you are relating will have the ability to project onto you. Other people may engage in such projection in an attempt to have power over your anxiety and the uncomfortable feelings your disquiet brings up within them. Only when you have moved through the integration phase and can be present with stillness and compassion do the people around you respond less and less to you and a given situation. There is no hook for their projection if you are acting from a place of stillness.

An illustration of this process would be if a soldier were preparing to go into battle, and his commanding officer who was about to call out the battle cry urinated on himself out of fear while standing in front of his unit. It would be difficult for the troops to follow the orders of their leader after witnessing a scene like this. In fact, it is known that a military unit will kill a new commander if they perceive that he demonstrates little or no courage and is afraid, for a panic-stricken commander will place the entire unit in danger from the enemy. Fear is a natural part of going to war, as it also is in the integration process. It is normal to be afraid, but can one be present with fear without it becoming overwhelming? And if it is overwhelming, can one just be aware? As my example with the doctorial students indicate, yes one can.

When you begin to work with an ego structure during the stage of acceptance, you need courage, as you are vulnerable. You are without defense against your fear that underlies the structure and that is readying for integration. You not only have to be present with your own fear, but you must also be present with the apprehension of not knowing what the result will be.

This is an unfamiliar world that you are entering, and a new way of being in the world that you are encountering. Such work requires bravery, for you have little or no defense to keep down the level of anxiety so that the individuals with whom you are in relationship and who have not integrated this structure into their own psyches are comfortable around you. Other people will try to draw your attention away from the integration process by creating difficult situations as a way of feeling more in control with your anxiety as you move with integration. Staying focused on the integration process and where you are in that process will assist you in coping with others' reactivity. Otherwise, you will be dealing with the dramas people initiate in order to distract you as a means of dispelling their own anxieties and, in turn, removing you from your own disquiet.

Faith

Many years ago, I attended a lecture by the spiritual teacher Ram Dass, at which he posed a question about the relationship between faith and grace. I had always viewed grace as the result of Integrative Consciousness, which is stillness, peace, and compassion with a situation. I began contemplating this connection, as I saw great value in Ram Dass's question. Then, an insight came to me and I shared this with Ram Dass. Faith is my relationship with God, and it is through my faith that grace is the result of God's relationship with me. Ram Dass pondered this thought for a time before responding that he too could see this relationship. My ability to understand the process of Integrative Consciousness, to see the results of a state of consciousness that includes no fear and has stillness of mind and clarity with an ego structure, and to witness the miraculous results enacted with clients and others increases my faith. So when the road gets a little bumpy and the struggles increase and multiply as the ego structure projects onto my external world in larger and more dramatic ways (typically through collective groups or important relationships), I can stay the course. I can affirm that this integration process works. The question becomes, can I find the strength to wait for grace to come in, for integration to occur, or for the pattern to fall away? The ego does not have control over any of these processes or the timing of these events.

Here We Go Again . . .The Cycle Continues

Another way to consider Integrative Consciousness—and a way that allows faith to be attainable—is to realize that patterns are cyclic. Just because you achieve Integrative Consciousness with a structure does not mean that you will not come upon that dynamic again. For instance, using the earlier example of criticalness that a man may encounter in a woman, he may confront this structure at the age of 28 in a dramatic way, in the form of his mother or wife, to the point that he may sever that relationship because he is unable to gain insight into his piece of the projection. After leaving the relationship, he may discover that he has found his independence and self-acceptance once again. The problem is that he has realized this outside of a relationship with a woman. Then, 14 years later, he may come across criticalness in the form of a female boss or partner. This time, the repercussions can be greater, because they might affect his job and employment status or a marriage. Yet he has matured in ego development and is now ready to see his part in the relationship he has with female power figures. Perhaps he begins the process of Integrative Consciousness and is able to resolve the inner conflict within his own psyche. Again, 14 additional years later, he might once more see criticalness (as this does exist) in another female boss. This time, he has little or no reactivity to this structure, for he has resolved his relationship to criticalness and approval. The way that he responds to a woman's disapproval has improved to the point that he makes absolutely no judgment; he has only compassion for the carrier of criticalness, that is, his boss. He may see her judgment of him as an expression of her own self-doubt and have a depth of understanding as he faces doubt in his own life and is transformed psychologically. The action he takes in exchanges with his boss can now address exactly what the situation calls for.

When you begin to see that patterns cycle and occur without any participation on your part, and when you start to witness the successful integration of your consciousness in your life, faith in your process and life in general increases. Integration of the ego structure does not mean you will not come across the pattern again. Integration of consciousness assures that there is not attachment to the pattern, that the relationship to the pattern has transformed, and that there only exists compassionate understanding and stillness when the pattern arises in our experience, again.

Meeting Your Dark Self on the Sacrificial Altar

When you have strength, courage, and faith, it is easier for you to maintain 'allowing'. By allowing a situation to occur, you permit it to unfold without intervening to manipulate the circumstances or the outcome, even as your defensive structure attempts to step in. Allowing 'what is' opens the door to acceptance. In the example of Dancing Bear, I permitted the situation in the classroom to play out while I maintained awareness from an observer state of consciousness. At the same time, my defense came in, in the form of my manipulating the group power through obtaining their sympathy. Yet I allowed the defensive path to present itself while I continued to observe, all the while understanding that I was not yet ready to hold the collective's disapproval without trying to shield myself against it. This is okay. Many individuals involved in awakening judge themselves when they are not compassionate and react with anger, anxiety, or sadness. When this occurs, they pretend to feel compassionate about a situation in which they are involved. This type of response is not in alignment with integrity for your process, and it denies the expression of vital aspects within you. Also, if you only pretend to feel compassionate, then you are simply caught once again with defense, adding another layer to the structure.

In the earlier example of the minicomputer project, my allowing myself to remain uncomfortable with my feeling of incompetence, or at times observing the defense I felt against my feeling of inability and helplessness, assisted me in that relationship until integration finally occurred. What is more, my being aware and letting in the prospect of failure, as well as permitting my defense to play out brought me into a deeper understanding and witnessing of these aspects. In my willingness to sacrifice an illusion of what my ego deemed as important (in this case, success), coupled with a growing faith in the greater order of things, I surrendered. As I let go, I opened up to Grace, or Integrative Consciousness. Allowing my ego to surrender itself to incompetence, failure, and helplessness began the process of Integrative Consciousness for me. Sacrifice is a necessary element of acceptance. Eventually, when the timing is right, the process of Integrative Consciousness occurs within us. However, until then, one remains in vulnerability and on the sacrificial altar as long as necessary. Thus, with the computer project, Integrative Consciousness brought about a change within me and new possibilities for the project, the company, and myself. Allowing from a witness state prepares the way for acceptance. Moreover, heart-centering assists a person in obtaining the witness, or observer, state of consciousness.

Heart Centering

After 25 years of doing my own consciousness work, I have not encountered a greater resource than the ability to focus at the heart. When we drop our awareness to the center of our chest (just to the right of the physical heart), it transfers our state of consciousness to the witness state. Such a shift begins to decrease the mental and emotional discourse inside us. The more we are able to sustain our awareness at the heart-center, the more we bring our psycho-physiological system into coherence, into an overall balance. As a result, we experience high levels of mental and emotional stability through increased synchronization and harmony between our cognitive, emotional, and physiological systems. When a person can pair this mind / body synchronization with his / her fearful duality structures, then this coherent synchronized system has an effect on an anxiety-provoking structure.

Some have described heart-centering as the center of your beingness or the center of centers. I see it as the portal to a place of balancing at that point where the unmanifested and manifestation of all of life meet. Heart centering provides the ability to transfigure from one state of consciousness to another.

Compassion and Unconditional Love, Attributes of the Heart

Heart-centered awareness innately carries with it two attributes of this state of awareness. They are compassion and unconditional love. Compassion is a form of energy that surpasses the emotional responses of empathy, pity, or mercy. Compassion is the ability to connect to your own suffering or that of another without experiencing the need to relieve that suffering. There is direct realization of someone's experience and no need to alleviate or manipulate their pain as the understanding exists of the purpose.

Pity and empathy are not compassion. In many cases, these emotions surface as a means for us *not* to experience the distress of another person, in other words, to place us in positions of control. When I drive past the homeless man begging for money, out of my pity or empathy, I may give some money to assist him in alleviating his suffering, but at the same time I am also alleviating my guilt about not being homeless. Thus, I have obtained some control over this aspect of my suffering. When I empathize with someone, I can feel or relate to that person's pain but also understand that he / she is the one who has to walk in those shoes. With compassion, I recognize that another person's pain is my pain. I, too, walk this path, though perhaps not in the same way or in the same depth as the other person.

The closest thing to unconditional love is the Mother's love for her child. Unconditional love is a love based on no judgments. It is self-less love. Unconditional love, an attribute of heart-centered awareness, assists an individual who is accessing this state of consciousness to come into a great healing balance with his / her own judgments. It takes one out of the personal and into understanding the fundamental relationship of things. It is the key of understanding the mystery of seeing the transcendental nature of temporality and manifestation, so that one can fully engage the experience. It is through unconditional love and compassion that one has the structure to break the spell of ego and its shadow, moving beyond duality and into the elemental relationship of things.

I have had a lengthy discussion about this subject with friends and colleagues in recent years. Can one reach that unconditional state with others? In our talks, we use an extreme example. Could you attain a state of unconditional love and at the same time live with a very bad and mean person? For if you are unconditional and therefore, not victimized by this person or the situation, then you could be with this person without the need to change him / her. You could accept that person as he / she is, knowing and understanding his / her struggles and inner conflicts. There is no need to manipulate or change that person, just love them. It is not the personal, egotistical love. It may be easier to find a level of acceptance when encountering this type of person on the street or in a gathering of some kind, but to live with someone such as this may be a different matter altogether and a state that only one could wish to attain. But if you are operating from compassion and unconditional love you understand your path with this type of person and the purpose this serves, not your ego but that of a larger good.

A metaphoric, introspective movie that demonstrates this theme is *Spring, Summer, Fall, Winter. . . and Spring* (2004). In this beautiful, simple cinematic expression by writer Kim Ki-duk, she describes the life of a boy as he explores his own violent nature under the tutelage of a Zen monk, who is a healer for a remote community. The boy comes to the monk as a baby. The monk raises the boy as his protégé and a possible candidate to inherit his position as healer, using the boy's own violent experiences to teach him of compassion and awaken truth within his student. When the boy leaves the small monastery for the love of a woman, the older monk is accepting although he grieves as his protégé leaves. The young man later returns as a grown man in his middle adulthood and is seeking the sanctuary and tranquility of his mentor. The older monk eventually discovers that his protégé has murdered his wife and his love out of rage over betrayal and jealousy. Yet, the monk continues to accept and live with the man who has killed, without any judgment. The protégé soon discovers for himself a moral and spiritual redemption for his actions of murdering his love through the guidance of his mentor. The monk has been accepting of the boy's and now the man's journey into violence, living first with the boy and then the man. The monk appears to have acceptance of and no attachment to his protégé, who may or may not, out of his own choice or inability, inherit his position in the community as healer. The monk's actions are, I find, the ultimate expression of unconditional love with attachment.

The Art of Heart-Centering
To use the heart-centering technique, find a quiet place where you will not be disturbed or interrupted. Have a conflict in mind for which you are ready for a consciousness shift to occur. For this exercise, we will use our previous example of feeling criti-

cized. Sitting in a chair, allow your awareness to go within as you close your eyes. Follow your breath, or use any other means that is appropriate as a way to relax the body, focus the mind, and calm the emotions. Then, begin by dropping the awareness, usually seated in the mind, down to the place that is above the sternum and rib cage and between the breast, at the center of the chest, to the right of the physical heart. In my own practice, I find it helpful to envision a ball of light at the center of my chest. Placing my awareness, or my mind's eye, there at the center of the chest, I then call upon the attributes of the heart—compassion and unconditional love.

Bringing in these attributes quiets the mind and calms the emotions even more. At this time, I then bring in the dynamic I am working on, for example, feeling criticized. If that is reflected in a person in my life, I can use the image of this person as a means to keep my focus on feeling criticized. If I am unable to identify with criticalness as a way of being for me, then I become in touch with my fear of being critical or criticized. I hold this in the essence of the heart-centered awareness with compassion for as long as I am able, maybe a few minutes. If defense begins to make its way in, it can arrive, for example, as a thought, 'But, Melissa, you are educated, you have a job; therefore, you are okay.' However, I do not allow this thinking to distract me. I acknowledge the thought and return once again to my fear and my feeling of compassion and unconditional love.

Research on Heart-Centered Awareness

Much of our understanding of the relationship between the brain and the heart is based on the idea that the brain influences the heart. Only rarely do we hear that the heart also influences the brain. This dialogue between the heart and the brain has been researched in a growing body of compelling evidence that has helped us understand the connection between the brain and the heart more fully. It is common knowledge that stress and our mental and emotional attitudes affect our physiological health and overall well-being. Long-term studies conducted by Dr. Hans Eysenck and his colleagues at the University of London have demonstrated that chronic, unmanaged emotional stress was six times as predictive of cancer and heart disease as cigarette smoking, cholesterol levels, or blood pressure (1988, 1991, 1995). Groundbreaking research by John and Beatrice Lacey (1978) showed that the heart communicates with the brain. The heart sends meaningful messages to the brain that it understands and obeys. These types of findings have led us to appreciate how the heart significantly affects the way we perceive and react in the world.

Extensive and revolutionary work has also come from the eminent brain researcher and neurosurgeon Karl Pribram. His work assists us in acknowledging the importance of the emotional system and its influence on the brain. In his model, Pribram describes how past experience builds within us a set of familiar patterns that become established and maintained in our neural networks. Input from our external environments and how we interpret those situations help maintain these networks and also influence us to react the same as in the past when we come upon similar circumstances that stimulate our interpretation of that situation (1993).

This study, I believe, supports the notion that change is difficult and requires diligence in practice, such as using the resources discussed in this book on a daily basis, maintaining awareness and acceptance, and staying in awareness and acceptance until integration occurs. Each small change creates new neural pathways and new interpretations and responses to the situations we encounter.

The Institute of HeartMath Research Center has explored the physiological processes by which the heart communicates with the brain, and how the heart influences the processing of information, perceptions, and emotions. The Institute has conducted

Head-Heart Entrainment

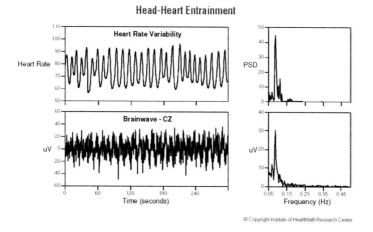

© Copyright Institute of HeartMath Research Center

Figure 1. The synchronization that occurs between the heart rate variability and EEG waveforms. Adapted from R. McCraty, W. Tiller, and M. Atkinson, 1996, Proceedings from the Brain-Mind Applied Neurophysiology EEG Neurofeedback Meeting: *Head-heart Entrainment: A preliminary survey.* Key West, Fl. (1996).

numerous studies involving the heart-centering focus, and their findings support the power of heart-centered states of consciousness. One study has shown that heart-centering has 'outcomes of reduced stress, anxiety and depression; decreased burnout and fatigue; enhanced immunity and hormonal balance; improved cognitive functions; and health improvements.' This investigation (McCraty, Tiller, Atkinson, Rein, & Watkins, 1995) found that when people learn to sustain a heart-centered focus with compassion, the brain can be brought into synchronization with the heart. The subjects of the study were trained in heart-centering techniques and learned to sustain this heart-focused state along with appreciation or unconditional love for a period of time. Heart-rate rhythms have greater synchronization and increased coherence to the brain while a person is in this heart-centered state (see Figure 1). The key findings of this research were that different emotions affect the autonomic nervous system function. Anger or fear tend to increase sympathetic activity, while appreciation is associated with a relative increase in parasympathetic activity.

Rhythms of the Heart

Another investigation revealed that a heart generating a coherent signal has a much greater impact on other biological systems than when it is generating an incoherent or erratic, chaotic signal (McCraty, Tiller, & Atkinson, 1996). The heart, when functioning in a coherent mode, will influence the other systems, the brain being only one system, assisting these systems into synchronization with its rhythms. This coupling of brain and heart rhythms demonstrates that heart-centering with compassion can quiet the mind as well as calm the heart.

I have recognized this synchronization in hundreds of my clients over the course of 18 years of private practice. What I have witnessed is that with consistent practice with awareness tools and heart-centering into acceptance, clients will soon experience a physical awakening if they have not had this type of experience before. Once a physical awakening has occurred (see Chapter 4 regarding my experience of physical awakening), then ego defenses become more intense and reflected in our physical experiences and made conscious by our understanding the projective nature of our ego. I have found that as the individual continues to practice awareness and acceptance through heart-centering methods, within a two-year period (typically), that individual experiences a large breakthrough consciously. I interpret this dramatic development as similar to my own experiences, in that as an individual progresses in his / her relationship to heart-centered awareness and meditation, then a trust in this relationship grows. I liken this process to the ego becoming more and more comfortable with releasing its need to control, so that it relaxes into the heart with less and less defensiveness. The deepening in the heart becomes greater and greater. The deeper the ego goes into this state of consciousness, then the quieter the mind becomes. Individuals reach this level of stillness in their meditations, and then the challenge becomes to raise oneself out of the chair and continue with this state of consciousness as they create in the world.

Heart-centered awareness is an easy way to maintain this level of consciousness within the chaos of life because all we need to do is hold our awareness (the mind's eye) at the center of our chest. Only the ego's state of unease with releasing control prevents a person from staying in this awareness. The ego may become fine with letting go of control while a person is sitting in a chair in a quiet room, but it certainly becomes another matter when that person encounters the chaos of life.

The research by the Institute of HeartMath is the beginning of scientific support for Integration of Consciousness processes. Moving into a heart-centered, observer awareness brings a person into a state of consciousness that is quiet in the midst of the chaos that occurs with consciousness transformations. The ego in its relaxed state will not need to reach for defense. The structure that is of a dual or a once-defended nature can now prepare for integration into the larger state of consciousness.

One further investigation (McCraty, Tomasino, Atkinson, & Sundram, 1999) involved the training of Sunnyvale, California, police officers in heart-centering techniques. This study indicated how quickly a person could return to a calm state of being after encountering acute stress if that person employed heart-centered awareness. I also believe this study supports a person's increased ability not to identify with the victim perspective during or immediately after engaging in a stressful situation (for instance, my encounter with Scary Ed). In this study, the police were used as control and experimental groups. The job of law enforcement exposes police officers to extreme levels of on-the-job stress. This 16-week study assessed 29 officers before and after a heart-centering training program.

They were evaluated in the areas of physical symptoms and vitality, emotional well-being, coping skills, work performance and effectiveness, family relationships, and their physiological and psychological recalibration following acute stress. Monitoring was used to obtain continuous ECG data throughout a series of simulated calls used in police training. Results of the study indicated that the officers trained in heart-centered modalities experienced reductions in stress, negative emotions, and fatigue, as well as increased peacefulness and physical vitality. In contrast, the control group showed minimal positive change and a worsening of stress over the same period.

One officer who was called to a domestic violence training scene applied the heart-centered technique to help decrease anxiety after the intense situation occurred. The research indicates that this officer had an immediate drop in heart rate back to the baseline. Without the use of the heart-centered method, the average time it took for an officer's heart rhythms to normalize was 1 hour and 5 minutes (see Figure 2).

The implication of this research is that from the witness, or observer, state of heart-centered consciousness, the response to stress takes place in the moment and is quickly released, and the mind / body system returns to normal functioning. From a consciousness perspective, one experiences the pain of the moment and lets go, thereby not becoming attached and developing a pattern of suffering.

Putting Theory into Practice in Relationships

In the next chapter we will look at the phases of consciousness awakening and the Integrative Consciousness Process in intimate relationships, discussed earlier in Chapters 5 and 8, and consider how to employ these techniques to support integrative consciousness. Chapter 11 explores this process in the context of my marriage and divorce, and demonstrates how the steps of the Integrative Consciousness Process can assist us in successfully

Acceptance

Heart Rhythm of One Officer Using Freeze-Frame
After the Domestic Violence Scenario

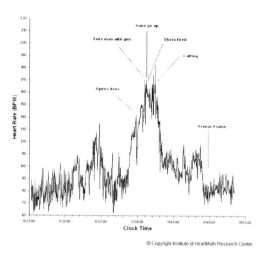

© Copyright Institute of HeartMath Research Center

Figure 2. The heart's ability to return to the baseline after experiencing
a traumatic event. The police officer involved here used heart-centering
modalities called Freezeframing. Reproduced from R. McCraty, D.
Tomasino, M. Atkinson, and J. Sundram, 1999, *Impact of the heartmath
self-management skills program on physiological and psychological stress in
police officers.* (Publication No. 99-075). Boulder Creek, Calif.: Institute of
HeartMath.

completing these stages.

To summarize my own experience in the phase already
discussed, the Emergence of Opposites stage of Phase One
occurred when I realized that stepping out into the world after
college with a bachelor's degree in psychology might be quite
challenging. I met my husband and I projected my psyche's
opposites onto him, which were strength, intelligence, and the
ability to make things happen. This projection served in assisting
me to take on the challenge of entering the world and making that
transition from my parents' house and college. As long as my
husband was at my side and the marriage strong, then all was

179

right.

In the next stage, the Bargain Stage, I made my agreement with myself: if I marry this man, he will keep me safe from the challenging world. I did not have much conscious awareness of this contract. I thought the only reason for the marriage was because I was in love. But the silent, unconscious marital agreement was made—he would provide and I would accept and love him.

The Betrayal and Disillusionment stage surfaced within the first five years of our marriage (typically it is about 7 years for a first marriage, hence the saying, 'the seven-year itch'). The betrayal stage emerged when I began to see that my husband was not holding up his end of the bargain, which he was not consciously aware that we had made. This is the stage in which I begin to explore the opposite poles of my projections of strength, ability, and protection. For example, I initially projected on him all the qualities unrealized within myself that I needed him to have in order to provide for me safely. When we graduated and began our engineering jobs, within a week he approached me. He said he was unable to do engineering and that he wanted to bag groceries for a living. He did not believe he was capable or educated enough to do this type of work. Bagging groceries is fine as an occupation, but it may prove difficult to raise and support a family on that type of income. I also sensed a faltering in his confidence, and because of my own level of ego development, I could not find compassion for his situation with work and his own struggles. I could only see this declaration of quitting engineering as a betrayal to our 'silent' marital agreement.

The stage was now set for consciousness transformation to occur if we had the strength not to get caught up with the illusions of our ego.

Chapter 11

Descent into the Unconscious

We must be willing to get rid of the life we've planned, to have the life that is waiting for us.'

Joseph Campbell

Phase II—The Descent

It had been four months since I had returned home from my Las Vegas trip described in an earlier chapter. Upon arriving home, I noticed things were different. Steve had swept the carpets and even done laundry, washing the bedding. I commented on the initiative he had undertaken, and actually felt this was his way of expressing that he had missed me while I had been away. Then within a week, I noticed changes in his behavior. He was working late, which was something he had never done either in the ten years of our marriage or his nine years with his company. His behavior toward me was not the same, either. He became irritable, snapping at even the most innocuous comments. The look he would give me was one that I would jokingly say he would only have for his mother, a look mixed with annoyance, anger, and, yes, hatred. I could not understand why this was happening. How had I contributed to this juncture we had come to in our marriage? I saw the reason for his distancing himself from me as something that I was not doing right, or as that I was somehow disappointing him and he did not want to be around me.

I began to apply the tools of consciousness awareness. Through understanding my projections, I tried to discern the quality of my relationship to the projections and to use heart-centered acceptance to be present with my fears and pain. At first, I employed these resources in an attempt to save my marriage and to manipulate the situation (a defensive structure), but these soon became the tools I needed to save my life.

In my effort to draw on these resources, for instance, when Steve would come home from work, I would ask what he wanted for dinner. Knowing that he liked pizza, although I was not fond of it, I would suggest ordering pizza. I wanted to please him. He would glare at me with his 'mother's look' and walk out of the room with no response. He then would leave the house and be gone until early morning. I could understand his leaving, as the tension in our home had reached such an intolerable level that it felt as if we were walking through molasses around each other. In my various brief interactions with Steve, I saw reflected what were beginning to be the patterns that were arising within me. One such structure was the fear I experienced in asking the simple question regarding the pizza. I was afraid of his displeasure, his rejection of me, and—something else that I had a difficult time understanding and that I feared—his disappointment in me. This latter conflict I would come into an understanding of its origins later.

Steve's going out during the evenings and into the night allowed me to sit in meditation. I sat, first, from a heart-centered space with my fear of rejection and displeasure, and then would sit with the feeling of disappointing this man that I loved. This meditation was difficult, for my anxiety was heightened by the unknown. I did not know what lay ahead. One possible, incomprehensible result of this contemplation could be a future that did not include my marriage. I sometimes would find only a few minutes of quiet meditation and presence with my fear before becoming very overwhelmed, losing focus, and ruminating about where Steve was and with whom. Those few minutes of calm and relief from my suffering during my heart-centered meditations were well worth the five hours daily I invested in this art of reflection.

I also understood that Steve appeared to have 'split off' his psyche. I was carrying for him the projection of his 'bad' mother, hence the looks he had been giving me. I understood that typically an affair can lead to this splitting of the bad and good mother, as the mistress will carry the aspects of the 'good' mother and the wife the dark aspects. Nothing I did on an outer level could change this. As long as I was overcome with fear, all my actions amounted to manipulation and a need for me to find control and a hook for my husband's 'bad mother' projection. He had always seen his mother as controlling. It made no difference whether I was nice and agreeable to anything he brought up. I was still the recipient of those 'mother' looks. He continued to see me as controlling. I also understood that my own fear lay beneath my actions of being agreeable and nice. Therefore, my behavior was not authentic. The way I was acting was incongruent with my feeling affect, thereby offering up that 'hook.' Steve would see my actions as controlling (rightly so, as I was trying to manipulate our relationship and Steve into what we had had before, so I could feel safe again).

What I could do, however, was understand that as I released my fears that were reflected in our marital relationship and did not take his actions toward me personally, acknowledging they were his own subconscious reflected onto me, then we could reach a place within the relationship where we could make a decision of whether to stay together or leave each other.

The Dark Side of the Heart
The control aspect was driven home when Steve and I went to couples counseling. We attended about three of these sessions before he refused to schedule again. But during one session, I was in my heart-centered space and sending compassion to Steve, again in an effort to dispel his anger, as he really did not want to attend these sessions. The counselor would check in with each of us. As he asked Steve how he was doing, Steve replied,

'Fine, if she would stop directing that heart-centered energy to me.' I was startled. 'How did he know?' was my first thought. Moreover, right on the heels of that thought came, 'This heart-centered energy is very real if he can feel it.' The counselor was taken aback. 'What do you mean, 'heart-centered energy'?' Steve darted me an enraged look and then shot back, 'Ask her.' I said that he was right. I was heart-centering and sending him compassion. Steve walked out.

I was left to truly understand how I had used the heart-center in an effort to manipulate him and how truly desperate I was at this point. This was not compassion. Instead, this was my using the observer state as defense. I became very careful from then on not to use heart-centering as a defense structure, or a means of controlling the situation. Using the heart-center as another means of defense would mean that I would become stuck, again. All I could do at that time was meditate in order to find clarity within my own psyche, releasing my own conflictual dynamics that were reflected onto the relationship.

In my interactions with Steve, I would listen to myself, especially when he shot the 'mother look' at me, to determine where I was in my relationship to rejection. The less and less I felt victimized by those looks, the more comfortable I was in being present with the fear of rejection. Listening helped me to maintain an observer state of awareness and assisted me in bringing my attention back to myself. I did not focus on what Steve was doing, as this would place my 'power' onto him and out of my control.

So, four months after my physical awakening experience in Las Vegas, I found myself curled up in a fetal position on the bathroom floor at 3:00 a.m. as wave upon wave of despair came over me. My husband, earlier that day, had told me that he no longer loved me. I asked if there was another woman involved, and he assured me there was not. I asked if he wanted a divorce, and he said he did not know what he wanted. I do not know what is worse: to feel unloved just for who you are, or to feel the rejection of your husband finding another woman that he sees as more worthy.

I was experiencing for the first time in my life, a situation over which I did not have any control or any say in what was happening to me. I was facing a collapse of my value and belief structures. The collapse was swift, just like the destruction of the World Trade Center Tower when hit by the terrorist piloting plane. Beliefs of my youth and young adulthood were shattered, left in the rubbles of my mind. Beliefs, such as the understanding that if I am good and good to people, then good things will happen to me, were no longer a truth of my consciousness. My dreams of having a happy marriage until 'death us do part' and of my future happiness with the man that I loved were threatened. I now found myself in an extremely helpless position. The only thing I could do was to curl up and sob until all my emotions were spent. I could not focus in the heart-center. I could not meditate. I was beyond my ability even to cope. I was at the apex of a crisis, caught up in the vortex of the chaos all around me. I was fully involved in a underworld process and I didn't care.

I came into the understanding that experiencing the acute pain of a situation as the situation occurs is actually easier then allowing the pain to form into a chronic suffering pattern. Acute pain becomes suffering when it is not experienced fully in the moment and becomes attached to previous similar painful events.

Deciding to End My Suffering

The next day, I came up with a plan to end my life and made a decision about how to do this. I would get into my car, close the garage door, start the car, and go to sleep. I did not tell anyone about my plan. I wanted no intervention to occur when I was ready to act on my plan. Yet due to the previous night of crying,

I was drained and had no motivation to carry through with my plan on the following day.

It is interesting how other people reflect back to you the different aspects of self. I had a set of friends that would angrily tell me to throw my husband's clothes out onto the lawn, change the locks on the door, and sell whatever possessions he had that were of any value. I understood that they reflected the angry, betrayed aspect of me, and when I wanted to feel justified or pretend I was on the high road, I would call these friends. Then I had a set of friends that would comfort me by saying that this was a projection of my ego and the necessary journey to grow spiritually and not be reactive, to see beyond the illusions of my mind. This outlook became difficult to understand, as my crisis was so intense that I could not perceive that what was occurring was an illusion. The pain and reality of the situation were too great. These friends were able to take me out of my emotional crisis and pain and into more awareness and a feeling of having more control, more into my intellect. Then, I had one friend, who would just be quiet with me, no comments regarding consciousness, no questions about my marriage, no anger or self-righteous attitude projected onto the situation, just an allowing and a trust in my ability to move with what needed to be moved with. She would walk with me in silence, not asking or commenting much, just being present with where I was at the time. All my friends were invaluable in helping me, bearing witness, and standing with me in what was, as for many women who go through a challenging situation in their marriage, a difficult and dark period.

I spent another night on the bathroom floor. This time, I felt the depths of helplessness intermingled with my despair. My cold bathroom floor had become my sacrificial altar. Nothing could rescue me now at this point. Not the knowledge that I had a successful career, not the excitement of returning to school to study psychology, which was my passion, not the realization that

I could support myself financially and that I had friends and would not be alone, not even my marriage returning to the state of love, respect, support, and happiness it had been before my Las Vegas trip. I had lost my innocence of life, and at this stage of desolation no ego-defense was able to rescue me from this place.

Moving into Phase III—Integration

Once again after hours on the floor, I was spent, exhausted from the outpouring of emotions, but something else was stirring. I was calm. Now, something else began to come through: hope. The next morning, I awoke and knew that I had reached a turning point, because I did not wake from a victim perspective as I had every day for the last several months. From the victim point of view, I looked at each coming day and wondered if I had the strength and fortitude to continue to go to work and focus enough to complete my responsibilities. I wondered if I was going to make it through the day believing my marriage was over and that I could not live without this man.

But this morning and every morning that followed, I felt strong, empowered. I looked forward to the day and what surprises it would bring. I spent the rest of the next day in heart-centered meditation, just being in compassion for myself. There was no sitting with fear, no attempt to manipulate the marriage or Steve, no effort to find clarity so that he would love me. I felt just unconditional love for the woman I used to be, the woman now trying to make her life work, and the woman undergoing a major transition reflected in the release of the self that had been in the 'old' marriage. I had just witnessed the death of Melissa, the first night spent on that bathroom floor.

Since this suicidal period in my life, I come to fully understand that suicide is an attempt, one last raise of the fisted arm to the heavens to say, 'God, I have the influence to decide my fate and I am taking it out of Your hands, as You don't seem to be doing a good job with it now.' I also know that suicide and its underlying push for control reflect the nature of the ego's surrendered release into that larger state of consciousness. From the ego's perspective, it does undergo a death in order for the event of integration to occur, the surrendering to something that has a greater authority, and the ego can and often does respond in rage. However, as discussed earlier, I could not allow myself to move toward this loftier representation of suicide. I needed to be in my vulnerability, present with courage and calling into myself all my inner resources to assist me. The dynamics underlying the suicidal situation—control, anger and violence—would later play out again for me in the situation involving Scary Ed as well as other situations not related in this book. I believe my ability to move into Integrative Consciousness during that hostage situation was the result of my having done the psychological work using the Integrative Consciousness process at this earlier stage in my life when I was feeling suicidal at the demise of my marriage.

Now the aim of my meditations was only for me to find clarity and peace within, as acceptance of what was and what is began to encompass my emotional state. I would sit with my fear of anger toward men (see Chapter 5), my fear of disapproval from the father, my fear of rejection from the man I loved, my fear of losing control, my fear of loneliness and of going through life totally responsible for myself, and my fear of living with the consequences of those decisions. I understood that life reflected back to me the structures my ego was resistive with or attached to, and that the next step was for me to free myself from those structures. I was letting my life show me the path to my consciousness transformations by my paying attention to and being aware of the situations, people, and objects that brought up a reactive response. Once I saw a family rollerblading in the neighborhood, and I felt the pain of the possibility of not having my own family that would do such an activity together. Later that day, I sat with my fear of not ever having family togetherness. I had attached myself to these ego structures out of fear. My goal now was to liberate myself from these fears that were not based in my current reality but rather in some fear-based future projection.

Being My Mother's Daughter

Not all of my awareness at this time was centered on my marital relationship. As discussed in Chapter 5, I would see my ego conflicts reflected in my relationship with the computer project and in the relationship with my boss. Another connection was also coming to the foreground that hit at the core of my self-worth. I had noticed that I wanted not to disappoint Steve and would sacrifice myself in order for this not to occur. I could not understand where the dynamic of disappointment was arising from. Up until now, I had not suffered any major disappointments in my life. Because this structure was in my relationship with my husband, who was male, I looked at my relationship with my father and did not see disappointment patterns in that relationship. The fear of disappointment would arise when I witnessed any distress in Steve. I wanted him to be happy with me, seeing me as valuable in his life. An example of how this pattern would play out would be when we were driving together and he would be angry at a car that had cut him off in traffic. He would yell at the other driver, and I would reach over and console him, providing a solution to his distress, such as telling him to drive around the other driver. This behavior from me surprised me. How could I be reduced to taking responsibility for actions and situations that were not my own? This anxiety of my not being enough for Steve and the fear of disappointing him were strong. I knew intellectually that this belief was ridiculous. Why would I take responsibility for my husband's happiness? But the intellectual understanding did not resolve the underlying feeling and my responses to triggers. I took this fear of not being able to please and of disappointment to the 'heart-center', breathing in the inability to please, breathing out unconditional love. I tried simply to be present with this fear of disappointing.

The full force of this pattern did not come into full understanding for me until later. I had just completed my doctoral studies, and my parents had attended the graduation ceremony, as had a few of my friends. After receiving my degree, I was standing in my cap and gown next to my mother and father. One of my dear friends approached my mother and said, 'I want to meet the mother of a most amazing woman.' My mother looked at her, appeared somewhat ill at ease, and said, 'Yes, but we always wanted that boy.'

My friend looked on, stunned, her gaze shifting to me, her eyes welling up with tears. She turned her head for fear that my seeing her hurt would initiate a crying episode from me. I felt my mother's comment cut through me like a sword. I experienced the pain of never being truly accepted or loved for who I am. I understood so much in that moment. I understood that, as the firstborn, the oldest of three daughters, I represented my mother's failure at providing my father with a first-born boy and the means to carry on the family name. I understood that all my successes would be a reminder to her of her failures and her own lack of power. I was doing things that would strike terror in the heart of my mother, such as working in business, graduating from college, taking vacations alone, having a failed marriage, and living away from the city where the rest of the family resided.

My own suffering and that of my mother were driven home even more sharply when a few years later, my mother gave me my baby photos and baby book. There, written on the first page, was the book's prompting question, 'What did your mother say when the doctor placed you in her arms for the first time?' Mom's written response was, 'I looked over at your Father and said, 'You are not disappointed she is a girl, are you?' Therefore, my first moment in this world had been met with regret about who I was, and all from the one person I needed to love me unconditionally. On reading this remark, my tears flowed and a compassionate understanding of who I am, my drives in life and some of the basis of my achievements, my relationships, and the difficulties I sometimes had with my mother all arose within me simultaneously. This core pattern runs deep within me, and usually is reflected in my intimate relationships, or relationships in which a power element exists.

I sat in meditation of this realization, feeling compassion for the newborn that had greeted the world and met disappointment from those who were to love her. Everything began to fall into place—an understanding of my marital strife and its purpose. All of these events were occurring at the time Steve asked me for a divorce.

Coming Full Circle in the Marriage

When Steve said he wanted to divorce, I sensed and understood that he had found another woman, a new mistress that he saw as someone he could spend his life with, even though he continued to see his original lover. At the time that he said he wanted to end the marriage, I was ready. It had been almost two years since my return from Las Vegas. I was prepared to step out into the world, in a new way, to experience what life was going to offer up for me now. I was now at peace with many of the dynamics that had caused me so much suffering and pain, especially after the last night I had spent on the bathroom floor. These dynamics were dropping away and no longer being reflected in our relationship. Initially, when my reactivity to one of his rejected looks that he would direct at me began to lessen, then he would up the ante, such as deciding to take some time alone for the weekend. Yet, each time I would see the fear, I would 'take it to the heart', raising the palms of my hands to the center of my chest, crossing one hand over the other, and dropping the awareness there. This symbolic gesture was my mudra, and this initiation into the heart was beginning my movement into compassionate awareness. The more I practiced, the more I reached a stillness with *what is,* especially after the realizations that came after the night spent on the bathroom floor. The more I continued to reach these states of calm, the more I saw Steve suffering.

I suspected he was experiencing pain, because it was becoming increasingly difficult for him to project onto me. My hooks were disappearing. I was approaching my new life as a single woman with excitement, not fear. I had come full circle, actually a spiraled circle back to the point of origin, except higher up. I was grateful that Steve had 'hung' in there with me long enough that I could complete this transformation, for he too was struggling with the hurt of the experience and the tension that had been in our home. He was the reason for my suffering and it was through my suffering that I was finding liberation from the structures that didn't work for me anymore and actually kept me from realizing a potential purpose. Everything that I had needed for my transformation had been carried in the container of the marriage. It had taken over ten years of marriage to build the energy required to 'blow my mind' into a new approach and way of being in the world. If Steve had left the marriage too early, then much would have been lost, as I would have needed years to work through it all, to have the tension that needed to build in order to break through the ego's defenses. I understood that Steve actually had to have his mistress as his distraction from all his pain. He did not have the resource of meditation and reflection and was not interested in this type of depth work. Somehow, he was the only person, along with the structure of our marriage, who could push me to face the intense suffering I had created and provide the impetus for me to enter the darkness of my subconscious. I would never have done it for anyone or anything else, not even for myself at the time. It was his gift to me, albeit an unconscious one on his part.

If I had approached this crisis in an ordinary state of awareness, I would have been either victimized or else dead by my own hand. The victimization could have taken on many forms, a need for revenge, deep anger and rage, thoughts of unworthiness, low self-esteem, or moving on to another relationship worthy of my dark projections. As it turned out, my marriage and subsequent divorce were my apocalyptic moment and not my catastrophic life event. I had unveiled and uncovered much darkness within my own psyche. I now had the courage not only to go through with ending my marriage but also to quit my profession in the field of computers and open a private psychotherapy practice, something unheard for a recent graduate. So the challenge I had faced at 21 years old, when I had looked at the psychology bulletin board and thought, 'How am I to make it on my own in the world with no job lined up in my field?' I now again encountered as a young woman who owned her own power and could undertake such a challenge. I had truly come full circle.

The Divorce Ceremony

Steve's and my divorce process was going along well. Very few discussions were involved, and there was no need for attorneys. We had no children, which helped, I believed. Steve agreed to our divorcing without hiring attorneys and putting our situation into an adversarial one by involving this third party. I wrote up our divorce decree, he consented to it, and then he hired an attorney to present our divorce to the court. The cost was $60.00 for the court costs and $90.00 for the attorney's fee. I attributed our ability to set up our divorce this way to the inner work I had done. I no longer felt like a victim in the current situation, I had resolved much of my anger toward Steve, and I felt a quiet within. I was looking forward to my new life as a single woman, and was ready to move on.

One of the difficulties I had with the legal divorce was

resolving the commitment and promise I had made before God almost 12 years earlier in our wedding ceremony. I needed some way to break this commitment and contract I had made at a sacred level. I thought and thought about what I could do, and then it came to me.

I asked Steve if he could be at the house (we both continued to live together, in separate bedrooms, until the house sold) that evening at the time of our wedding ceremony, which had been 6:00 p.m. I told him that I wanted to do a divorce ceremony, that I wanted him to participate in it, and that I would appreciate it if he could do this one last thing for me. He agreed. I let him know I was making the plan up as I went along, and that if he wanted to contribute anything to the ceremony, he could. I asked him to wear his wedding ring. He agreed to what he thought was a simple request.

The night of the ceremony, I prepared by lighting 12 candles in the form of a circle, one for each year of the marriage. I found our unity candle and placed it in the center of the circle. I laid tapered candles next to the unity candle. I took a ribbon from my bridal bouquet and placed it in the center of the circle, along with a pair of scissors. I had a photo taken right after our marriage vows that I also put in the center beside the other things. I located the most spiritual music CD I could find, which happened to be a pipe organ piece that sounded like the grandioso overture of 'The Phantom of the Opera'. Maybe not appropriate, but I wanted something substantial.

Steve arrived right on time. His face registered a look of shock or horror when he first heard the pipe organ music and then saw the darkened living room, lit only by the 12 candles in a circle. It appeared that his mind was thinking, 'What kind of witch spell has this woman placed on me, and will I live to see another happy day?' His eyes darted around, either taking it all in or else looking for an escape door if one should be needed. He said, 'I didn't prepare anything.' I responded, 'Oh, that's okay. This is our ceremony, and we can do whatever we want as it moves us.' He seemed to become at ease with that statement.

We went to the center of the circle and sat next to one another. I then began to perform the wedding ceremony in reverse. I picked up our picture and cut it so that the couple became two separate individuals. I selected the ribbon next. Steve held one end and I the other, and I cut the ribbon, signifying the breaking of the tie between us. I explained the symbolism of each action, although no explanations were needed, as both Steve and I understood the significance of every act. We picked up the tapered candles and lit them from the unity candle, placing the lit tapers in their holders and then blowing out the unity candle. By this time, tears were streaming down Steve's face, and he was wiping them away as quickly as they fell. It was the first time I had witnessed his vulnerability since we had entered into our marital crisis. Now, we removed the rings from our fingers, saying the marital vows in reverse and doing the best we could. Steve then decided to share all the happy and special moments we had had together. I shared a few memories. I was crying at this point, too, for all the experiences that had gone before us, and for what perhaps could have been but was not to be.

The next day I felt significantly different. I was lighter. I was smiling. I was not back to normal, as that 'normal' would never exist for me again. I was a different, a more alive 'normal'. People whom I knew approached me asking if I had lost weight, changed my hairstyle, or if I had some happy news to share. I had not discussed any of my marital problems or divorce with many people, just close friends. Now I was able to share because I had such stillness around the situation. My calm that was at the base of my demeanor took many of these people by surprise. They had had no idea about my troubles and were curious as to why I was handling the divorce so well, especially since Steve had initiated it. I had never realized the power of ritual to access that part of the psyche that is beyond thought and emotions.

Nevertheless, who I was that day, I could only attribute to the power of that ritual to heal.

Later in the week, Steve attempted to pull me back into the marriage. I reminded him that we were actually legally divorced. I recognized he was feeling the complete separation that the ritual had provided us and that the legal divorce could not bring about. Another week later, to the surprise of our realtor, the house that she had said would take another year to sell, according to the market analysis, sold, and at our asking price.

I was finally free, light-hearted (in more ways than one), following the rhythms of my heart and with my eyes seeing a bright future with no pretense that it would not contain its challenges, but ready and excited to start again. And that future delivered.

Chapter 12

Resonance

Personal transformation can and does have global effects. As we go, so goes the world, for the world is us. The revolution that will save the world is ultimately a personal one.

Marianne Williamson

This chapter deals with the fourth component of the Integrative Consciousness Process, resonance. Resonance allows us to take on the suffering of others, holding a space of compassion for them, and to discover compassion for our interpretation of their suffering. The quieter we are in our relationship with another's suffering, the more assistance we offer to the other. By holding a stable, still, compassionate relationship to another's suffering, we begin to provide a healing space and a space of no fear in which the other person can also begin to transform his / her suffering. The other person realizes he / she is not alone in the pain.

A research study by HeartMath supports this connection between individuals (McCraty, Atkinson and Tiller, 1999). In this investigation to determine the effects that one individual's heart rate has on another's brain waves, the findings were astounding. What researchers discovered is that when two people are sitting within conversational distance from each other, the heart rate of one will influence the brain waves of the other. What is more intriguing is that when the 'listener' is in a heart-centered space and he / she is generating a coherent heart rhythm, then synchronization with the other's brain waves is more likely to occur and at greater levels. The implications of this study are obvious. When listening from a heart-centered state of consciousness, we are open in our vulnerability and strength and are providing a transformative effect on another who might be suffering in his / her experience.

A Daughter's Loving Gesture

When my father developed dementia affecting his recent and immediate memory, I practiced resonance. One particular instance stood out. I had been sitting in heart-centered meditation with my own fear of losing my mind, the projection I was placing on my father that I experienced when around him. I wanted to prepare myself so that I could be fully present without anxiety when I visited my father during the last stages of his disease. Dad and I were sitting around the breakfast table when he suddenly had this worried, frightened look on his face. He said, 'I know I just had my coffee cup in my hand and the next second it is gone.' My mother quickly jumped in to reassure my father that he was just dreaming, a popular response from full-time care-givers. I leaned toward my father, recognizing the fear of uncertainty, the fear that one's mind is slipping into insanity and I placed my hand over his, saying, 'It must be frightening to see your coffee cup in your hand one minute and the next it is gone.' My father sighed and looked at me with tears in his eyes and said, 'Yes. It is awful to live this way sometimes. I have to remind myself it is the disease and look around me for something familiar. It is sometimes too scary to even talk about it with anyone.'

As we engage in this practice, it not only provides a healing space for the person going through a painful experience but also for ourselves, as we are transforming our relationship with the underlying dynamic of our own suffering that is reflected in the other. We begin to take back the projection of the suffering and thus can end the perpetuation of this energy. In this way, we can start to offer service to humanity by holding a space for the suffering of others who are struggling to carry this suffering themselves. By our altering our connection to the structure that underlies another's pain, a change occurs in the propensity for this structure to be projected out either by ourselves or by others. For example, if we are able to find stillness with greed, then this allows others to transform their own relationship with greed. The more individuals transform this relationship of greed, then the less this structure, that is, the fear that underlies greed, needs to be constellated at the collective levels, such as through the Bernie Madoffs or the AIGs of the world.

Challenges do occur when we begin to carry another's suffering. One test you may face is that you may also be victimized by allowing yourself to become too vulnerable while being present with the suffering of the other. You too may begin to enact the dynamic. In this case, you have become victimized by the suffering and the underlying structure because your psyche has a powerful need to have a more direct experience. Below are two examples of resonance. Both demonstrate the potential for transformation—the former, a real-life example, and the latter a theme from a popular movie.

Carrying Another's Unconscious Dynamic

One of the more loving examples of resonance I have ever witnessed occurred with a couple that came to my practice for counseling. I shall call them John and Diane. They were both in their early 30s. The first time I saw Diane was when she entered our offices of the Mind / Body Connection, without an appointment. She was agitated and crying uncontrollably. Her eyes were swollen and red, and she was wiping away tears with a wadded up tissue she clutched in her trembling hand. In between sobbing, she told me that she was on the verge of an emotional breakdown, needed help, and did not know where else to go.

Without going into detail, she relayed a tale about having to face dynamics of violence and control elements from the age of

16 and on. She had been in remission for multiple sclerosis and interstitial cystitis, the latter a disease that allows toxins to penetrate the bladder wall, causing extremely painful urination. Both diseases reflected her patterning of life situations regarding control dynamics. She was fearful that her MS was coming out of remission, as she had begun to have symptoms. On top of all of this, her marriage was encountering difficulties.

As I sat listening, I wondered if I would have to arrange hospitalization for Diane, because she was being overwhelmed with her anxiety. As she told her story and I stayed present, I had to be attentive to my own reactions to her suffering, as well as listen to her and her reactivity, which helped to calm her down. I agreed to see her in my practice and planned to introduce her to heart-centering in the next session, which we scheduled for the next day. If she was not able to use this technique to calm and stabilize herself, then we would decide whether she would need to be admitted to the Emergency Room for a psychiatric evaluation.

Fortunately, she returned much calmer the next day, as she felt she had a plan to address her anxiety and that she would be able to use the heart-centering technique. By our third session, Diane was prepared to proceed with the task of uncovering the underlying dynamics that were reflected in her disease and caused her extreme stress.

Within a short time, she went back into remission with the MS, which I thought was remarkable. I could sense Diane was only able to hold a heart-centered focus briefly, for she was unable to shift into the depths of the terror that resided underneath her disease. This is understandable, as she had just been introduced to the heart-centered modalities and did not have much experience with transformative work that would allow her to develop the levels of trust needed to move into those deeper levels. Diane's dynamics around violence and control ran deep within her consciousness, and the fear on her part was great. She had a hard time holding these structures in the space of her awareness even while in a heart-centered consciousness. When psycho-spiritual dynamics reflect metaphorically at a physical level through disease, the intensity or depth of the pattern is considerable. It takes an expanded consciousness to maintain these dynamics in awareness or with a degree of stability within the psyche. (For an interesting study on the psychotherapeutic approach to physical illnesses and the clients' perception of those illnesses, refer to the article by Broom [2000].)

After I had a few sessions with Diane, her husband wanted to meet me. He was curious about the person who had introduced his wife to a new approach to living her life. He has seen the initial results of Diane using this meditation technique and was amazed that she was becoming calmer without the aid of medications. Diane gave permission for us to meet. John came to my office. He was a genuine, mild-mannered man. He had a smiling, upbeat personality and enjoyed joking with people. He loved his wife dearly, as was evident in how he spoke of her respectfully and with concern. Although, I was picking up a similar anxiety within him as I had noticed in Diane—an anxiety around control—he appeared to be enjoying life in the moment. I was also able to recognize in our encounter that he was afraid of losing his wife and living life without her.

Within a few short months, I noticed that Diane was in full remission, her visible symptoms having completely disappeared. She stated she was feeling great. Her life began to reflect this upturn in her physical health, for she began creative projects and spoke of returning to school.

Then she told me that John was having problems, such as dizziness that made it difficult for him to walk without falling. He was seeing a specialist to determine a diagnosis and hopefully provide a cure. They both were hopeful that there would be a simple explanation, maybe an inner ear problem. Diane understood John's anxiety around his illness because she remembered her own concern about her initial symptoms of MS and how within a short time after her diagnosis she had gone blind in both eyes. She related what a terrifying experience that was for her. Diane asked me to see John in order to teach him heart-centering as a way of decreasing his anxiety. I agreed to do this, and John and I set up an appointment.

John at this time had taken a leave from work, and he looked like a completely different man when we met again. He was pale, and his motor behaviors showed a trembling of the upper and lower extremities. He had to hold on to furniture as he walked hunched over, or lean on Diane in order to make his way to the chair. I was amazed at how this healthy man could deteriorate within a few short months. He continued to be upbeat and hopeful regarding the condition of his health.

Then John began to use the heart-centering technique and started to work with his relationship with his unnamed disease. Within a short period of time, he was having difficulty seeing because his eyes were now light sensitive and he had to wear light-blocking glasses all the time. Before long, John had decompensated to having to use a wheelchair, as he was unable to stand without falling over.

As part of the treatment plan of working with this couple who had very similar unconscious dynamics, for John also had patterns surrounding control and violence in addition to one issue that was somewhat different from Diane, that is, abandonment, I told each partner to be aware throughout his / her day of what was being projected out onto the screen of his / her life. Diane was to pay particular attention to her projections with John, for he was now holding her relationship to her disease and her control dynamics. I indicated to Diane an insight I had that as long as she was in relationship with John, then her disease would remain in remission. It was demonstrated that she did not have to experience the disease by taking it on in her body for her consciousness process. For her, the dynamics underlying her disease could be experienced by being in relationship with a person having a similar disease dynamic.

The next step was for the two of them to discern their relationships with their projections in order to provide feedback as to where each person was in the integrative process. Then, through heart-centering meditations, they could be present with the underlying fear. The more they were able to do this, the more the quality of their relationship to their diseases would change, resulting in an improvement in their day-to-day experience with their illnesses. The goal of treatment was not to heal the disease but rather to find a depth of understanding of the dynamics surrounding the disease. Releasing the internal conflicts around their illnesses which include a deepening of awareness and acceptance for what is, begins the process of changing his / her relationship to this debilitating illness.

What occurred was that Diane soon wanted out of the marriage. As she began the separation process between herself and John, an interesting development resulted. Diane came out of remission. I do not know whether she remembered my insight a few years before, but she quickly decided that she would make her marriage work for now. As she re-entered into the marriage her MS returned to remission. Both Diane and John decided to remain married and to continue their consciousness practices.

This relationship dynamic brings up interesting questions. Did John take on a disease that reflected the psychic conflicts of the couple when Diane could no longer cope? Did he do this out of unconscious, unconditional love for his wife? I have witnessed a number of relationships such as this that have reinforced for me the wonder and mystery of marriage or these deep level commitments.

What Dreams May Come

There are times when movies reflect the deeper themes or movements of consciousness and collective unconsciousness, whether or not this is the deliberate intention of the writer or the director. *What Dreams May Come* (Ward, 2001) is such a movie. It exemplifies the component of resonance. The story line is about a young couple, Chris and Annie Nielson, who lose their two young children in a car accident. The pair struggle with the emotional devastation of their loss. Annie goes into a deep depression and is hospitalized in a psychiatric ward. Chris, who deeply loves his wife, has a difficult time with Annie's depression. He is unable to deal with her darkness. He visits her at the hospital and tells her that today is 'D' day, meaning he will either divorce her or she will have to do whatever it takes to pull herself out of her depression, and then they can continue on with their lives, together. Chris says he cannot go on like this anymore. He wants to live his life completely and not in the darkness of Annie's despair. Annie, fearful of losing Chris, agrees to put aside her distress, and so denies herself the grieving she is feeling, in order to make the marriage work. A very short time later, Chris dies in an auto accident. Annie, alone, cannot survive the loss and commits suicide.

The movie now moves to the afterlife. Chris finds himself in an astonishing, beautiful place, where his thoughts alone manifest his reality. He is truly happy. He soon discovers that Annie, after her suicide, is banished into a different, dark, desolate, pain-driven realm of her own creation, as she was filled with despair upon her death. Chris decides to risk his own eternal happiness to rescue Annie from her self-imposed world. What occurs next in the movie and what the director, Vincent Ward depicts so well in his direction, are the steps one must take to have resonance for another person.

Making a Heartfelt Connection to Another

In order for Chris to find Annie, he must hold an image of her in his mind. This strategy establishes a connection and brings Chris into close proximity to his wife. He is now on the edge of her dark world. In our own lives, when we turn our attention to a friend, family member, or stranger, we begin the process of connecting to that individual. We are bringing their image—who they are and their fears and love—into our inner world. This process occurs automatically, and typically on a subconscious level, meaning that we are unaware that we are taking in so much of an individual. What happens in most cases in which awareness does not exist in either party is that we begin to relate to that individual from a defended ego. We have sympathy or pity or sadness for that person and his / her plight. These are defenses against the suffering of the other. Such defenses serve us well because our ego is unable to be present in our vulnerability to the other person's experience. However, great growth, both spiritual and psychological, awaits us there.

Another important part of connecting to another individual is to establish this connection from a heart-centered focus, which allows a witnessing, or observer, state to come in. We can therefore be more aware of the dialogue occurring between us and the other person. That is, we grasp the deeper essence of the communication, and thus we can avoid 'taking on' the other's fear or underlying anxiety. Our sensitivity to the other person is increased. When we are open to compassion and unconditional love, then the healing pattern is activated for the other person, as well as for ourselves.

In the film, when Chris locates Annie, she is living in a desolate, run-down structure, vaguely reminiscent of her family home. Everything in the scene appears in tones of grey and has a hollow, empty sound. This scene is reminiscent of Dante's depiction of purgatory in the second book of his *Divine Comedy*. Annie does not have any of the comforts of her formal life. She is experiencing total fear.

The Risk of Resonance
Chris is warned by his mentor not to enter or stay in Annie's house for more than a few minutes; otherwise, his psyche will be

overwhelmed and he will risk becoming lost. If this happens, then Chris will remain in her world forever. Her reality will become his reality. This is the challenge for Chris, as he has to be fully present with Annie to remain at her side. In order to accomplish this, he must take on her reality; he must connect to her through her dark and depressed thoughts and feelings. Chris is willing to accept this challenge, believing that he may be able to reach Annie and assist her in leaving her dark and eternal existence.

As a therapist, I too allow myself to go to the places in which my clients reside. Yet I do this from the heart-centered focus so that I can maintain a centeredness with the challenges and fears clients wish to discuss and resolve in their own experience. I am acutely aware of when I am unable to hold this centered state with a client because when I am centered, I feel a grounded stability within. When I cannot stay centered, or when I sense an anxiety arising within me as the client relates a story, then I need to reschedule the session. This approach allows me time to sit in my own meditations around a client's dynamics (that are also my own) in order to feel the stability necessary for healing. I need to work with my own fears around the dynamics presented in session before I can hold a space for another to enter into their depths of exploration.

HeartMath's research (McCreary et al.,1997; McCreary et al., 1999) asserts that when one person listens to another from a heart-centered perspective, then the centered individual hears the other one with clarity and focus. This clearness that results is partly due to the lowering of the person's own mental chatter, but it is also an acknowledgment of more and more subtle aspects of communication. Subjects in these studies indicated that they became aware of the underlying essence of the other person's communications. I have found this to be true of my own experience as well.

Making the Connection

Returning to the discussion of the film, as Chris begins to take on the suffering of Annie, he finds himself at her side. He tries to offer up a reason so that she may be able to break through her darkness. This tactic fails him, as she remains in her dark reality. This scene depicts Chris's defense against Annie's suffering. He wants her to release her darkness so that he does not have to experience it. We are reminded of an earlier scene in the movie when Chris visits Annie at the psychiatric facility, where he tells her he is unable to live with her depression. Now he must make the decision to live with her depression even if it means doing so for eternity.

Surrender

Chris does have one thing going for him, and that is awareness. He understands that Annie's reality is only an illusion of her own making. Yet, he is also aware that her reality is stronger than his own, as it continues to exist. Her reality prevails even though Chris and his wife have moments of breakthroughs, depicted by Annie remembering good times she and Chris experienced on earth. Yet, the darkness wins out. Chris decides that he will spend the rest of eternity with Annie in her dark world. This is something he was unable to accomplish during Annie's psychiatric admission. Chris surrenders and takes on Annie's complete darkness that soon becomes his own. This utter giving in represents the final stage of the ego before integration occurs.

Integration

At Chris's surrender, Annie is no longer alone in her darkness and suffering. She recognizes Chris and remembers his love, which opens a doorway for her to begin the ascension out of her darkness. As she begins to break through, she is able to assist Chris to find his way out of his dark reality. They both are in the world of their creation, one of beauty and light and the other of loved ones. This reflects the integration and the new experience of wholeness and light.

Resonance-Extending to Others

Resonance is the final step of the Integration of Consciousness process. It is the ability to see the suffering in another, take on that suffering within one's own psyche, hold the tension of the opposites, or the awareness of the fear, and be present with this awareness until transformation occurs. The ability just to hold the suffering of another person within one's consciousness provides a service to humanity, for the other knows he / she is not solitary in whatever struggle he / she is facing. When a person understands he / she is not alone, it is easier to gather the strength, take the hand of the individual willing to brave the darkness, and be led into the light of wholeness.

Integration of Consciousness practices assist individuals in moving away from a catastrophic occurrence within their own psyche. Practices involving awareness and acceptance promote the ego's movement into integration. The momentous coming of the Self into conscious realization can be either apocalyptic in nature or can have disastrous results. A terrible outcome could be a situation in which all that remains from the aborted transformative event is ability to live a small life in fear. In terms of the broader world, daily apocalyptic events are occurring. They are manifesting at the collective level in the breakdown of our religious, government, financial, and social structures. Individuals can influence the results of these destructive forces by not allowing such events to have catastrophic endings. We must not turn a blind eye, and we must resist a war-like stance or the urge to crouch in fear. People can be greatly influenced by answering their own call to consciousness. Disaster for a person can only occur if his / her ego remains alienated, antagonistic, closed-off, distracted, and defended against the reality of his / her awakening consciousness that is manifesting into his / her world.

If that person's ego is courageous, open, vulnerable in its strength, permeable to change and to the search for the truth, then this can result in the person achieving wholeness, with no need to project his / her darkness out onto the world.

References

Almaas, A. (1986). *The pearl beyond price: Integration of personality into being, an object relations approach.* Berkeley, CA: Diamond Books.

Bain, B. (Producer), & Ward, V. (Director). (2002). *What dreams may come.* [Motion picture]. United States: Universal Studios.

Brooks, J. L. (Producer), and Crowe, C. (Director). 1996. *Jerry Maguire* [Motion

Broom, B. (2000). Medicine and story: A novel clinical panorama arising from a unitary mind / body approach to.... *Advances in Mind – Body Medicine;* Summer 2000 *16*(3): 161-179.

David, L. (Creator/Producer), and Seinfeld, J. (Producer). May 19, 1994 air date. *The Opposite Episode. Seinfeld.* [Television series]. United States: Network, NBC.

Edinger, E. (1994). *The mystery of the coniunctio.* Toronto, Canada: Inner City Books.

Franz, M.-L. von. (1980). *Projection and re-collection in Jungian psychology: Reflections of the soul.* La Salle, Ill.: Open Court.

Grossarth-Maticek, R., & Esenck, H. J. (1988). Personality type, smoking habit and their interaction as predictors of cancer and coronary heart disease. *Personality and Individual Differences, 9*(2): 479-495.

Grossarth-Maticek, R., & Esenck, H. J. (1991). Creative novation behaviour therapy as a prophylactic treatment for cancer and coronary heart disease: Part I–Description of treatment; Part II–Effects of treatment. *Behaviour Research and Therapy, 29*(1): 1-16; 17-31.

Grossarth-Maticek, R., & Esenck, H. J. (1995). Self-regulation and mortality from cancer, coronary heart disease and other causes: A prospective study. *Personality and Individual Differences, 19*(6): 781-795.

H. Read, M. Fordham, G. Adler, Wm.McGuire. Princeton:

Princeton University Press, 1953-1979.

Hesse, H. (1961). *Siddhartha*. New York: New Directions.

Joy, B. (1997). *Sacrifice and grace*. Lecture, Preston, CO.

Jung, C. (1966). *The Practice of Psychotherapy, The collected works of C. G. Jung*. (Vol. 16). G. Adler, & R. F.C. Hull (Eds.). Princeton: Princeton University Press.

Jung, C.G. (1959). *Aion*. C.W. 9ii.

Jung, C.G. *The Collected Works* (Bollingen Series XX). 20 vols. Trans. R.F.C. Hull. Ed.

Kongtrul, D. (2005). *It's up to you*. Boston, Ma: Shambhala Publications.

Lee Seung-Jae. (Producer), & Ki-duk, K. (Writer/Director). (2004). *Spring, summer, fall, winter . . . and spring*. [Motion picture]. United States.: Columbia-TriStar Home Entertainment.

McCraty, R., Atkinson, M.(1997). The electricity of touch: Detection and measurement of cardiac energy exchange between people. *Proceeding of the Fifth Appalachian Conference on Neurobehavioral Dynamics: Brain and Values*, Radford, VA, Lawrence Erlbaum Associates. Mahwah, NJ.

McCraty, R., Atkinson, M., et al. (1999). The role of physiological coherence in the detection and measurement of cardiac energy exchange between people. *Proceedings of the Tenth International Montreux Congress on Stress*, Montreux, Switzerland.

McCraty, R., Tiller, W., & Atkinson, M. (1996). Proceedings from the Brain-Mind Applied Neurophysiology EEG Neurofeedback Meeting: *Head-heart Entrainment: A preliminary survey*. Key West, Fl.

McCraty, R., Tiller, W., Atkinson, M., Rein, G., & Watkins, A. (1995). The effects of emotions on short-term power spectral analysis of heart rate variability. *Journal of Cardiology, 76*(14): 1089-1093.

McCraty, R., Tomasino, D., Atkinson, M., & Sundram, J. (1999). *Impact of the heartmath self-management skills program on physio-*

logical and psychological stress in police officers. (Publication No. 99-075). Boulder Creek, Calif.: Institute of HeartMath.

Perry, C. (1997). Transference and countertransference. In P. Young-Eisendrath & T. Dawson (Eds.), *Jung* (pp. 141-163). Cambridge, UK: Cambridge University Press.

Pribram, K. (1993). *Rethinking neural networks, quantum fields and biological data.* Lawrence Erlbaum Associates Publishers: Mahwah, N.J.

Siegel, D. J. (1999). *The developing mind: How relationships and the brain interact to shape who we are.* NY: Guilford Press.

Tolle, E. (1999). *Power of now: A guide to spiritual enlightenment.* Novato, CA: New World   Library.

Tolle, E. (2005). *The new earth: Awakening to your life's purpose.* New York: Plume.

Vincent, M. (Producer/Director), and Arntz, W. (Author/Producer). 2004.

What the Bleep Do We Know!? [Motion picture]. Beverly Hills: 20th Century Fox Home Entertainment.

Wachowski, A. (Writer/Director) and Wachowski, L. (Writer/Director). 1999. *The Matrix* [Motion picture]. Burbank, Ca.: Warner Bros. Pictures.

BOOKS

O is a symbol of the world, of oneness and unity. In different cultures it also means the "eye," symbolizing knowledge and insight. We aim to publish books that are accessible, constructive and that challenge accepted opinion, both that of academia and the "moral majority."

Our books are available in all good English language bookstores worldwide. If you don't see the book on the shelves ask the bookstore to order it for you, quoting the ISBN number and title. Alternatively you can order online (all major online retail sites carry our titles) or contact the distributor in the relevant country, listed on the copyright page.

See our website **www.o-books.net** for a full list of over 500 titles, growing by 100 a year.

And tune in to myspiritradio.com for our book review radio show, hosted by June-Elleni Laine, where you can listen to the authors discussing their books.

mySpiritRadio